The Strong Leader's Hand

The Strong Leader's Hand

6 ESSENTIAL ELEMENTS
EVERY LEADER MUST MASTER

DANIEL YORK

BookVenture Publishing LLC
1000 Country Lane Ste 300
Ishpeming MI 49849
www.bookventure.com
Hotline: 1(877) 276-9751
Fax: 1(877) 864-1686

Ordering Information:
Quantity sales. Special discounts are available on quantity purchases by corporations, associations, and others. For details, contact the publisher at the address above.

Printed in the United States of America.

Library of Congress Control Number	2017939987
ISBN-13: Softcover	978-1-946250-76-6
Pdf	978-1-946250-77-3
ePub	978-1-946250-78-0
Kindle	978-1-946250-79-7

1. Leadership 2. Character 3. Motivation 4. Vision 5. Attitude 6. Conduct 7. Teamwork 8. Discipline

Rev. date: 04/17/2017

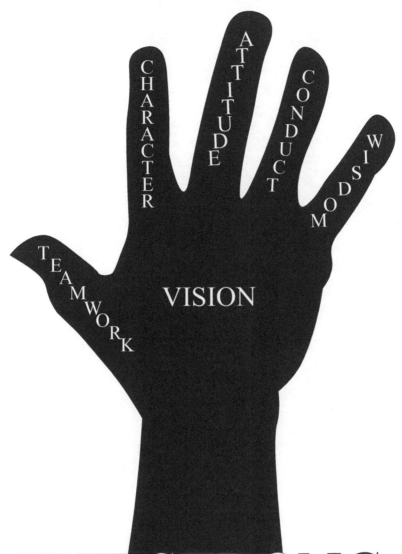

THE STRONG
LEADER'S HAND

Also by Daniel York

I Keep Asking

I Pray Also

Something to Think About . . . in Reveration

Climbing Higher . . . in Reveration

Lost on Mount Fuji . . . and other true stories

The Weak Leader's Fist

Dedication

This book is specifically dedicated to the men and women of the United States Army Cadet Command (USACC) and the 104th Training Division (LT), who tirelessly and effectively train leaders on and off our college campuses to serve our nation in all walks of life. More generally, this book is dedicated to all those who faithfully aspire to be strong leaders.

Special Thanks

Special thanks to Dr. John George and Sandy Ingrassia for their help in editing. Both provided stellar observations and attention to detail. Dr. George brought formidable experience as a leader and a student of leadership. I am grateful for his contributions.

Contents

Introduction

Authority can shape what a person does, but influence shapes who a person becomes.

—Erwin Raphael McManus in *Chasing Daylight*

It was a crisp fall day and the three of us were hungry. I had a *vision* for pizza and as I shared my yearning, my two roommates, Bill and Fernando, quickly nodded in agreement. Somehow it was decided that I would be the runner. I thought my *character* was sound that day as I set out to Tony's Pizza, that celebrated place where pizzas and calzones came to life below the clock tower. Certainly my *attitude* was positive. I was happy to go and pick up food the three of us craved. Up until that fateful afternoon, my *conduct* at West Point was exemplary. But that would change quickly as I came bolting into Tony's and saw all around me *only* upperclassmen. Slowly heads turned and too many eyes in that room seemed to fasten on me. Something stirred in my brain—that queasy, sick feeling that I was not supposed to be there.

Before I could turn and flee, a stern voice addressed me, "Mister, what are you doing here?" No witty reply leaped to my mind for this unknown inquisitor. He asked my name to which I am sure I replied, "Cadet York, sir!" He asked what company I was in, to which I am sure I said, "Sir, Company A-3!" What happened thereafter I cannot recall except wondering what punishment I would meet. It seemed the *teamwork* of three plebes to combine their money for a pizza was all for naught. Had we taken the time to read our regulations, we would have discovered that Tony's was off-limits to fourth classmen.

The demerits I received were rather light but, as word of my escapade spread, I became the butt of what seemed every upperclassman's twisted humor for the rest of the year. As I passed by senior cadets in the hallway, I would occasionally catch the snickering, "Hey York are you going to Tony's today?" It was a question of mirth that tested my mettle. But it also created camaraderie and reminded me to do my best in a place where leaders are forged for a lifetime of service.

West Point prides itself on producing leaders. But leadership is not something merely taught; it must be defined, applied, refined and wisely administered. In this book I will define what a leader is, explain why I chose the adjective *strong* to describe the leader, share why I use the hand as the instrument of illustration, and note contrasting styles leaders use.

This book is written primarily for all aspiring leaders who want to improve their leadership skills and, thereby, make a difference in the world. Specifically, I hope that this writing will be a helpful primer to those who will lead in the most unforgiving and exacting of all professions; the military. Through the past three decades of serving in both the military and civilian sector, I've studied many tomes on leadership, observed firsthand great and not so great leaders, and sought to master (sometimes well and sometimes poorly) the six elements that I'm about to share. These elements, when properly understood and applied, create strong leaders. Each of the six elements is linked to the hand and layered with true stories so as to make them easier to remember.

By way of a disclaimer, I must add that leading is an evolving skill and I am often reminded of how much I have yet to learn. I share personal observations and convictions in this book with which you may disagree. Please remember, my intent is not to gain unanimous consent. My hope is that this book will cause you to think and reflect and, in the process, become an even better leader!

Before I go through this journey of examining the strong leader, it would be wise to define what a strong leader is.

> **Definition of a Strong Leader:** A strong leader is someone who faithfully unites heart and mind in honorable, selfless action for the betterment of others so as to effectively accomplish the mission.[1]

I encourage you to consider the following questions in studying this definition.

1. Why is selfless action important?

2. Why do we focus on the betterment of others?

3. For what reasons (positive and negative) do people choose to follow leaders?

4. For what reasons do people choose to stop following leaders?

5. What facilitates the joining of heart and mind for a leader? And why are both essential?

6. How does a leader effectively focus so that the mission is clear and accomplished?

7. How does each of the six essential qualities of a leader fit in this definition?

I chose the word *strong* as the key descriptor for the leader. *Strong,* by definition, will directly apply to every element discussed in this book. Consider the following facets: *especially able, competent, powerful in a specific field or respect* [vision]; *powerful in influence, authority, resources, or means of prevailing or succeeding* [teamwork]; *of great moral power, firmness, or courage* [character]; *mentally powerful or vigorous* [attitude and wisdom]; and, *moving or acting with force* [conduct].[2] "Strong" should not be construed as heavy in the oppressive sense. Each of the fingers work carefully together to make a productive hand.

There are numerous ways to depict or illustrate a leader, incorporating the six elements. After many great suggestions, I chose to go with the hand because each of the elements is then naturally linked and, without any one digit, the hand is impaired. How well we put these six components together determines the *strength* of our grip. Strong leaders connect vision, teamwork, character, attitude, conduct, and wisdom to produce outstanding results. We neglect any component at our peril! The more wrinkled the hand becomes, the more selective we should be about what we do. Not everything we put our hand to is appropriate or successful. Life is a journey—not meant to be rushed or taken for granted. With this in mind, it is time to examine the six essential elements every strong leader must master.

Chapter One

Vision—The Hand at Work

Vision: Influences the *direction* and *commitment* of leadership.

Vision is the ability to perceive the action and resources necessary to reach a desired end state. Strong leaders recognize that vision is essential to move people or groups of people to do what is necessary to achieve success. Vision affects:

- *who* is recruited, educated, and empowered;
- *what* an organization will do;
- *how* it will go about its business;
- *where* an organization will go or remain;
- *when* transformation should occur;
- *why* people should engage in the activities or work they do.

Essentially, vision influences the direction and commitment of leadership.

What you put your hand to reveals what's important in your life. Let me emphasize again, *what you put your hand to reveals what's important in your life.* Metaphorically and in actuality, what you put your hand to represents your vision. To reach a place of solid leadership, we must understand and embrace vision! Have you ever served a leader without vision? Who pops into your mind? Was serving that leader valuable and good for the organization? Have you ever served a visionary leader? Whose image comes into your mind? How did this leader influence the organization?

There are *four important facets* related to vision. *First, it is crucial we craft a vision that is sound and enduring.* In March of 2011, when a devastating tsunami wiped out the low-lying communities along Japan's northeastern shore, one hamlet remained quite safe. In the town of Aneyoshi, a single centuries-old tablet was inscribed with the following words: "High dwellings are the peace and harmony of our descendants. Remember the calamity of the great tsunamis. Do not build any homes below this point." Because of their ancestors' vision in understanding danger, the villagers in Aneyoshi built their homes on high ground and were untouched by the great wave.[3] A significant piece in sustaining a sound and enduring vision is the creation of goals that encompass and wrap the vision so that all who are involved can bring it to fruition. We want to set SMART goals:

Specific

Measurable

Action Oriented

Realistic—challenging but achievable

Timely—set a specific time for the goal to be completed.

Microsoft's vision once read, "A personal computer in every home running Microsoft software." Notice how simple, yet enduring, this statement is. Furthermore, it is crafted in such a way that goals may be established to achieve its stated purpose.

Second, assuming that the vision is appropriate and clearly formulated, *we have to effectively communicate it.* What good is it to have a vision if people don't understand it? Cal was interviewing to be the executive director of a nonprofit organization. Along with his résumé, he submitted three one-page proposals of initiatives he would bring to the organization if they hired him. He was the only candidate to do this and as Ed, the current chairman of the board related, not only did the organization hire Cal, they knew from his initiatives what his focus would be and this led to over fifteen years of successful leadership.

Effective communication requires frequent reinforcing. Fumihiko Imamura is a professor in disaster planning at Tohoku University in Sendai, the city badly damaged by the 2011 tsunami. He noted that far too many people were killed by the tsunami because they forgot how dangerous it is to live in low-lying areas. It only takes about three generations for this to happen. The great-grandchildren don't hear the story.[4] Along the coastline of Japan there are many tablets like the one in Aneyoshi. Unfortunately, the vision for keeping people safe was not reinforced and, over time, disregarded. A forgotten vision is no vision.

Third, we have to obtain buy-in. Most people naturally resist change. It is not necessarily easy to win the hearts of people to a vision. People oppose change for many reasons. They may be tired. They may lack confidence or trust in their leaders. They may feel unappreciated. So, not only is it important to communicate vision clearly, it is also essential to gain the hearts and minds of those we serve so they are willing to be part of our team.

My West Point roommate, Dave, was selected to lead an organization where many on the staff were advancing in age. Dave recognized that for the organization to grow and be vibrant, he needed to bring in new leaders and to recruit new staff. In order to accomplish buy-in, he announced up front that he would serve five years with the intent that a younger leader would replace him. By doing this, he personally modeled the seriousness of his intent. This further increased his credibility in asking older leaders to step aside. To his credit, Dave actually did as he said he would—stepping aside after five years of leading. Dr. John George opined that your walk talks and your talk talks, but if your walk does not talk louder than your talk talks, nobody pays any attention.

The fourth facet regarding vision is that we must hold it with an open hand. Vision does not always turn out the way we planned or hoped. We have to be willing to let our vision adapt and grow. I grew up with parents that worked for an organization called the Navigators. It is a nonprofit organization of members committed to sharing the good news about Jesus and helping people grow spiritually. Eleven of my first sixteen years we lived overseas in Okinawa, Korea, Japan and the Philippines. Consequently, before I left to attend West Point and serve in the military, it was my personal vision to join the Navigators and live and work in Asia. My plans and goals were clear. Have you ever been in a place in life where you were pretty sure you knew what you were going to do?

In 1986 I left the military to join the Navigators. Six months into our training in San Diego, all the people who recruited me and were responsible for our training left. I call it the *ministry of abandonment!* The departing leaders moved to their new assignments, leaving me with the need to find another source for training.

During the next three years, my wife Kathleen and I stayed in San Diego, and I enrolled in a local seminary in order to complete a master's degree. Our first two children were born in La Mesa, California while we continued preparing for what I expected to be a career serving in Asia. Shortly before graduating from seminary, I traveled to Thailand to coordinate a short-term mission trip. My folks lived in Bangkok at the time and, after spending a week with them, my dad asked me if I would come over to Southeast Asia and serve as a Navigator leader in one of the nations there. That request was the culmination of my dreams. He was, in effect, *handing* me my vision.

The night following dad's invitation, I could not sleep. I spent miserable and frustrating hours tossing and turning, knowing that something was wrong. I got up the next morning and told my father that at that point in time I could not say "yes." I returned home very unsettled as to what my family should do.

Months later, Kathleen and I attended a party at Dana Point in San Diego with a Sunday school class that I was teaching for young married couples in our church. Our three-year old son Bryan was walking robotically on the sand. We took him in for testing and Magnetic Resonance Imaging (MRI) from the neck down but the results showed no problems. However, within months, Bryan's eyes began to cross. His eye doctor told us to get him to a neurologist immediately!

On Valentine's Day, 1991, Kathleen and I walked into Doctor Schultz's office. The first words out of his mouth were "Mr. and Mrs. York, you need to sit down." I don't know about you, but when I'm told to sit down, the information that follows is never good. So I stayed on my feet (which didn't help). As kindly as possible the troubled doctor told us: "I'm very sorry, I don't really know how to tell you this, but your son has a brain-stem glioma. It is an inoperable and fatal tumor. There's nothing we can do. He has *maybe* a five percent chance to survive."

In March and April, I took Bryan to a radiation facility for a total of 72 treatments. Twice a day for 36 days, we drove from our apartment in National City to San Diego, so he could lie still and be zapped. Bryan was so cooperative that he never required anesthesia and the nurses loved him!

Now I have to interrupt this story to ask several pertinent questions: Was my vision to move overseas at this point realistic? No it was not. Who was in control? Not me.

My vision collapsed—it had little chance of succeeding with Bryan's situation. What I thought I was going to be able to do literally dissolved. I remember one Sunday standing in the parking lot of the church we attended crying my eyes out. I looked up and said, "*God, what is it You're doing? If You want to take our son, it's okay, because You made him. I'll still follow You, and I'll still love You, but what is the point of all this?!? What are we supposed to do?*" I was in the middle of a dark cloud with no idea when the sun would shine again.

One of my seminary professors called me in April and told me about a church in Oregon that was looking for a pastor to start a new church. He suggested I turn in a résumé. I am sure I must have thought, "Have you *forgotten* my circumstances! *I've never pastored a church in my life, let alone started one. My son is dying! What part of this don't you understand?* But, because there was nothing to lose, I did what he asked and mailed out a résumé.

Soon thereafter, I received a call from Oregon. The leaders of the church liked my application and wanted to interview me. Unbelievable! In May, I flew up to Oregon to meet with their search committee. I had one of the most relaxed interviews of my life. Essentially, I told them that if they hired me, they were making a mistake. I explained to them my family's situation. The prognosis of Bryan living was bleak. I told them about my shattered vision and the reality that I had absolutely no experience starting a church. (Growing up I used to have friends suggest to me that I should be a pastor and I thought *they* were crazy!) Regardless of my disclaimers, the men interviewing me were friendly and kind. We had a great discussion but I left fairly confident that I'd never hear from them again.

In June, I received a phone call. It was from the pastor of the church in Beaverton. Rick said, "Dan we selected you and we want you and your family to move up here and start a church!" Now at that point in time, Kathleen and I decided that if they were brave enough to take a chance on me, what were we going to do? How could we say "no"? Only God could set up something this insane and make it work! Rational people don't do things like that. What company in their right mind would have hired me?

Our lives were about to go in a completely different direction. When it comes to vision—hold it with an open hand. If you want your organization or personal life to succeed, be open to the fact that the vision may have to change. Life is not static. Circumstances and events often cause us to reevaluate and shift what we think is important. Personally, I entrust my life and the lives of my family to God. I believe His leadership is paramount and that His will is sovereign. I had to die to my own vision before I understood His vision for me. Amazingly, as a four year-old, Bryan's brain tumor was miraculously healed. He should have died but God had other plans for his life as well!

Depending on who or what you believe in will impact your understanding and execution of vision. So be wise and keep an open hand! The question now is, "What will you put your hand to . . . ?"

Terry de la Mesa Allen (nicknamed "Terrible Terry Allen") was given a colossal challenge. This flamboyant, charismatic leader almost saw his career end after he was relieved of commanding the First Infantry Division in Italy during World War II. Yet, because he was such a fierce fighter who instilled a warrior spirit in his men, General George Marshall asked him to take command of the 104th Division, known as the Timberwolves.

Major General Allen knew from experience in Africa and Italy that the Germans were ferocious opponents. So he took an innovative approach to training. Before his division shipped to Europe to fight, Allen insisted that his men train at night. At a place called Camp Carson, Colorado, the 104th Division conducted nightly maneuvers and exercises. Finally, the Timberwolves deployed to Europe and advanced through fighting across France, the Netherlands, and Germany. The 104th repulsed several fierce German counterattacks late in 1944 and 1945.

To prevent high numbers of casualties, General Allen often told his men to put their bullets away, fix bayonets and pack grenades! They were fighting at night. Then they audaciously attacked without firing their rifles or machine guns. If they heard a weapon go off, they knew it was a German firing at them. Pity the poor soldier who fired his weapon at them! He faced Timberwolves proficient in fighting in the darkness.

The 104th Division fought 195 straight days in combat. No division in the history of the United States ever accomplished such an amazing feat! Because Terry Allen was such an innovative leader, countless lives were saved! He understood something precious called *vision*. By the end of the war, the 104th Division was considered an elite fighting force winning a reputation as the nation's premier night fighters.[5]

Now let's move forward from World War II to meet a man known as Terrill K. Moffett. TK grew up in Amory, Mississippi, the youngest of nine children living in a home with no running water. Before he left home, three of his brothers died from muscular dystrophy. His father was a carpenter and was often away working. He was also an alcoholic and when he got drunk he often was both mean and violent. Before he returned home from work on Friday nights, he went out drinking. Family relatives hid the children in a pasture so their dad would not find and abuse them. When TK was only seven-years old, his father took his own life with a gun in the family living room.

Holding the family together was a very God-fearing mother who did her best to help her children succeed. Amazingly, she was not even allowed to drive a car or vote. With her encouragement, TK worked hard in school and in sports—motivated to be the best. One year he read thirty-five books and turned in reports for each one—so many that the teacher asked him to stop. In the 7th grade he decided he wanted to go to West Point. In the 11th grade, using an old broken typewriter, he typed letters to his congressmen expressing his desire to attend the Military Academy. Through his perseverance he received nominations to Annapolis, the Air Force Academy and West Point.

In 1971, Cadet Moffett graduated from West Point and received his commission as a Second Lieutenant. For five years he served in the active Army and then he joined the Mississippi National Guard. Eventually he was promoted to the rank of Brigadier General and then to Major General along with selection to command the 104th Division.

Those of us who served at the time will never forget when Major General (MG) Moffett came to Fort Vancouver, Washington, and first walked through our headquarters. Pulling all the leaders together, he looked us in the eye and said, "This place is a pigsty! Clean it up!" He could see something that the rest of us could not see. He had fresh eyes. We were used to working there every day. We didn't see the clutter and mess he saw. He quickly got our attention and put us to work cleaning, throwing out trash, painting, and changing the entrance to the headquarters building so it faced the parade field.

MG Moffett did not like to spend much time in his office. He preferred to be out in the field where the soldiers trained. He knew that he would learn more about the needs of his command by getting out with the men and women he served. While spending time watching the soldiers of First Brigade train, he was approached by some frustrated drill sergeants. At that time they wore on their dress uniforms a unit crest. It was a little blue bird called "The Fighting Marlin." Their active duty counterparts constantly teased the 104th reserve drill sergeants every time they wore those birds on their shoulders. Of course that did not go over well with them. MG Moffett didn't like it either. So, do you know what he did? He had his talented aide-de-camp design a unit crest that reflected the night fighter heritage he learned from reading about General Terry Allen. Two times he submitted the new design for approval and each time it was rejected.

Eventually, after careful research, his staff discovered that part of the old crest design traced back to the Crusades. Knowing the Crusades were politically incorrect, TK traveled to the Institute of Heraldry Historical Society and convinced them to support the new design. The Army G1 (Personnel Officer) was the approving authority and fortunately happened to be TK's West Point classmate! The crest was approved. Now the drill sergeants were able to wear a symbol they could take pride in and MG Moffett began sharing the Night Fighter legacy. Wherever he went to speak or to present his commander's coin for excellence, he told the story of the Timberwolves spending 195 consecutive days in combat.

Two men both saw the potential in the organization they served through innovative vision, instilled pride, a fighting spirit, and the professionalism that won worldwide recognition. Vision encompasses believing in your calling and knowing what your mission is. Make sure you carefully consider what you are going to put your hand to and communicate clearly with those who follow you so they know the direction you are headed and the priorities that will make your journey successful.

Major General Moffet was not just my leader; he was a friend and mentor. Through his influence and tutelage I one day had the privilege of commanding the 104th Division. In taking command of what was now a one-star command, I had to make an immediate decision. Should we focus on providing training and instruction for cadets at universities (ROTC) or on officer education (ILE)? We could not do both. Knowing that our future as a division was in jeopardy if we focused on officer education I elected to select the ROTC mission. With a vision of enhancing the regular Army's Cadet Command by providing professional reserve instructors and trainers we secured a stable and rewarding stake for ourselves and secured our future viability. Today, the 104th Training Division plays a pivotal role in the education and training of cadets across the United States.

Dave Knapp was a team leader for thirteen people for about two years. According to Dave it was two of the hardest years he experienced to that point. They were in a highly measured industry but were ranked 8th of the 8 teams in his area and 53rd of the 55 teams nationally. Having just terminated and replaced two problem employees that started with the team, he realized that they should be able to perform better.

Each person was very capable, hard working and success-driven. Several of them went through the difficulty of the last two years with Dave and now there were several new members that brought fresh energy and drive. He realized that both as a team and individually they needed something to rally around, to focus their attention and build pride in their team. Over the next several years the organization was poised to go through a lot of growth and, if they wanted it, each team member had potential and could have opportunity for higher responsibility. They would only be considered for promotions or other positions if they had a successful track record.

Dave believed in this team and each team member. He knew they were good, could achieve success and had potential for higher roles. This spurred him to create a vision to move them from their lowly 8th and 53rd positions to gain first place in their geographical area and to be ranked as one of the top ten teams of the entire organization within two years. To meet this vision, Dave framed out key areas of focus to bring his vision to reality. First he shared with each member his plan at a team meeting. Pairs or individual team members were assigned a key area and asked to outline specifics of what they needed to do individually and as a team in that key area for them to improve their performance. They also developed contingencies to anticipate change and possible failures in reaching some of their lofty expectations. Personal commitments were made so as to help them succeed.

After that meeting the vision and personal commitments became the drumbeat of conversations. If an individual could not fulfill a commitment, another team member was asked for help or to occasionally pick up the slack. Regularly members discussed successes, issues, and challenges, and made adjustments to their tactics and strategies. Through a lot of hard work, the team achieved the rank of first place within their area after only thirteen months and then ranked first in the entire organization after the fourteenth month! More impressively, they maintained those rankings through the next two years and into the third year. By achieving such remarkable success, Dave's team members earned promotions and transfers and were in turn replaced by new high performers. For Dave this whole experience reinforced how crucial it is to use vision with a clear strategy to deliver results!

Chapter Two

Teamwork—The Thumb

Teamwork: Influences the *magnitude* of leadership.

The thumb (teamwork) as it overlaps the other fingers in gripping, is a good reminder that we need each other. Perhaps this is even more fittingly illustrated by the handshake. A leader can have all the tools to be effective, but we must remember that we need the cooperation of people to succeed. It is the agreement between leaders and followers to work together and to trust each other that makes organizations safe, resilient, and prosperous.

Teamwork is the joint effort of a group of persons committed to the success of a shared cause. As such, it influences the magnitude or extent of leadership. It is a beautiful thing to watch people unite around a common goal to achieve something valuable. But as sure as the sun in the sky will sink in the west, there will always be challenges to teamwork. The earth does not lack for cantankerous, selfish, and mean-spirited people. Nor does everyone have the same views, strengths or energy to contribute.

Patrick Lencioni, in his book *The Five Dysfunctions of a Team*, shares valuable insight strong leaders must harness if they are to successfully lead teams. *First, leaders must lead in modeling vulnerability.* As noted earlier, humility and the willingness to learn are two vital attributes of effective leaders. Leaders who are vulnerable are particularly skillful in ridding their teams of an absence of trust; a condition that can paralyze an organization.

Second, strong leaders overcome team members' fear of conflict by demonstrating the ability to both allow for disagreement and to teach their subordinates or peers that decision-making is actually improved by inviting dissenting views. Artificial harmony actually stifles creativity and productive ideological conflict.

Third, strong leaders erase a lack of commitment by team members by holding to goals and established standards. An often overlooked aspect of maintaining standards is the practice of conducting rehearsals. Before making presentations, or conducting drills, or engaging in activity that is critical to the organization, rehearse what steps need to be taken, who is responsible for each step, and what behavior or action is essential to meet the established goals and standards.

Fourth, strong leaders tackle difficult issues head-on. They do not tolerate team members who deliberately damage the organization by their unethical or inappropriate attitudes and behaviors. They will take the appropriate measures to counsel and, if necessary, fire disruptive employees. In every war, soldiers are removed from duty because they malinger, steal, or are cowards. It is no different in peacetime. Organizations are comprised of people, and not every person is a good employee. The danger for many leaders is that they are wary of creating conflict. Often teams suffer because the boss is not willing to do the hard work of removing disruptive workers. Conflict avoidance is the easy course and usually the wrong course. Passing on "problem employees" to other organizations instead of just firing them is a cowardly technique that just ensures other people on other teams will suffer. Failing to correct wrong behavior actually can embolden the offender and make the work environment an unsafe place. Teamwork is best accomplished when each team member is made accountable for his or her behavior and belongs and serves according to the needs and mandates of the organization.

Fifth, strong leaders focus on collective outcomes. Rather than let each team member pursue personal goals or status, the wise leader directs the focus of each member towards the overall objective.[6] However, to get to a collective outcome, strong leaders also focus on the strengths and not the weaknesses of their valued members. Unfortunately, too many leaders assume that the best way to help their team is to correct the weaknesses or failings of their subordinates. This causes unnecessary stress and promotes conflict. No one wants to look bad or fail or get crushed for personal weaknesses. Nor does making a person a "project" so as to "fix" him, usually work. Wise leaders learn as much as they can about their teammates and then focus on their strengths. This motivates people to do even better and allows them to be recognized for what they do well.

I add a sixth component that is: *strong leaders work hard at building and sustaining solid relationships.* Too often leaders focus on work and productivity and miss the underlying need to establish meaningful relationships with their subordinates, peers, and superiors. If people suspect that they are merely "means to an end," resentment is sure to grow. Here are two examples that illustrate this:

Every week, almost without exception, we receive newsletters in the mail from people we know in nonprofit organizations seeking money. When I look at who the sender is, I make an immediate decision. If that person has never taken the time to call or write us and see how we our doing (relationship building), I throw the letter in the trash. Conversely, if we know the sender to be a friend who has made the effort to invest in our lives, Kathleen and I are eager to read what was written and to give to whatever the expressed need is.

My wife and I visited an organization for the first time and we were greeted soon after arriving by a couple that was very friendly. They spent considerable time chatting with us and we were quite taken by their warmth. Later they asked if they could come over to our house and visit. Just before it was time for them to leave, they revealed they were involved with a multilevel marketing business and asked if they could share it with us. Immediately we understood why they were so friendly. Now if this seems judgmental on our part, consider that after we politely turned them down, from that day forward they paid us no attention.

Strong leaders do not "use" people, they invest in them. Relational building does not mean that a leader must be "buddies" with everyone. Familiarity can breed contempt. However, investment is the leader taking and making the time to know those with whom he or she works. Leaders, who demonstrate they truly know as much as they can about their teammates and care about them, create a legacy of success.

As leaders it is our responsibility to value those we work with and to ensure we provide them with the tools they need to succeed. Thus we must differentiate between knowing what is bad and must be removed, from what is a weakness and must be overlooked. The better we know our people, the better we will be able to harness their skills and bypass their shortcomings. Sergeant First Class (SFC) Luther Tookes pulled me aside as a young lieutenant and told me that the key to successfully leading the platoon was to get to know each and every one of my soldiers. As I watched him at work each day, it was obvious he practiced what he preached. Ever since, I have worked hard to become familiar with the people that I serve. It is surprising what we can learn when we take the time to get to know our teammates. Well-functioning teams are so smooth that often it is easy to overlook the hard work and effort expended to grow each person to succeed.

Are you making the people around you better? Are you able to work with others? Do you let your teammates take the credit for success and build them up? Or is life all about you?

My sister Barbie is a wife and mother to four children. She is the quintessential "fun mom." Often her home is filled with kids from up the street who come over to skateboard, jump on the trampoline, or just hang out with her children. Barbie works the night shift at Meridian Park Hospital. While on duty one night, a patient's blood pressure dropped dangerously low. Barbie called the doctor and shared the sick man's vitals and the doctor wrongly replied, "You are overreacting—just give him fluids." But the man was clammy, pale, and retaining fluids. She knew his condition was deteriorating so she called a *rapid response* which means within minutes a supervisor, respiratory therapist, pharmacist, ICU nurse, and the head nurse all arrived. Fortunately, they were able to help the patient's blood pressure rise. Like me, you might wonder why in the world five people were needed for a drop in blood pressure. So Barbie explained to me: the supervisor checks the overall condition of the patient the respiratory therapist administers oxygen the pharmacist ensures the amount of drugs dispensed are proper the ICU nurse gives the drugs the head nurse helps wherever needed

Most hospitals in the world may not have the ability to assemble a rapid response team but the fact that this hospital can is important. Each of those five persons has a key role. With five sets of eyes, the possibility of identifying the cause of the problem and prescribing the right solution improves dramatically. The team works together to ensure a safe solution is implemented.

———————————

Have you ever heard of Ranger School? Ranger School is the toughest school the Army has to train its soldiers—short of actual combat. If you are in the infantry, you need to go where it's toughest. You want to be molded through fire. Fresh out of West Point, and after completing Officer Basic Training, I volunteered for Ranger School. In November of 1981, Class 2-82 began. We had to go through three phases consisting of training at Fort Benning, Georgia; the mountains of Dahlonega, Georgia; and swamps in Camp Rudder, Florida. The training lasted about two months.

Somehow I injured my Achilles tendon and, when we got to the mountain phase in Dahlonega, it became very painful just to walk. At many points the pain was so bad I seriously wondered if I could make it. One of my ranger buddies had personal experience in gutting it out through pain. Often, as if he could sense my mood, he would get right behind me on patrols and quietly say things like, "Don't you even think about quitting! Suck it up, you can make it!" His consistent encouragement was all I needed to keep going. One morning as we prepared to patrol on a particularly steep area, our ranger instructor (RI) told us not to put our field jackets on because, even though the cold air was dense, after we hiked we would start sweating and that would cause us to get wet and potentially suffer hypothermia when the temperature dropped.

At the time, I weighed probably 120 pounds. I am sure I was the lightest ranger in that class. I had virtually no body fat and I was cold! I remember thinking, "*To heck with you RI! I'm cold! I'm putting my field jacket on!*" So I wore my coat, and off we went up hills steep enough to make great ski slopes. I focused more on the pain in my tendon and did not think much about the fact that I was quickly warming up. Before long, I began to sweat and I had to take off my field jacket.

Hours later when we set up our patrol base, the temperature dropped below freezing and sure enough I started shaking. I could not get warm and I knew I was experiencing the onset of hypothermia. Now I had a choice to make. If I alerted the RI to my condition, he would have to order us to make a fire, which would compromise our security, and cause the patrol leader to fail his graded mission. If I didn't tell the RI, there was a good chance I would freeze and potentially die.

Knowing the risk, I chose not to say anything and hoped that somehow I could make it through the night. Mark Cole, a member of the Second Ranger Battalion from Fort Lewis, and also part of our squad of ranger candidates, saw what was happening with me. He came over to me and took his poncho and his poncho liner (all we had for warmth) and placed them over my poncho and liner and then laid on top of me until I got warm and was out of danger.

I'm pretty sure Ranger Cole was cold. He was not the patrol leader that night and he did not have to help me. But he was my ranger buddy and ranger buddies take care of each other at all costs. As if that was not amazing enough, Mark did something else I will never forget for the rest of my life.

Throughout our training, everyone sooner or later was assigned to carry a machine gun or a radio. Now remember, I didn't weigh much so having to carry a machine gun (M60) or a radio (AN/PRC77), each of which weighed about 20 pounds, along with a rucksack, ammunition, and water, meant I was exhausted. In mountainous or swampy terrain, extra weight made it very difficult for me to keep up with a patrol. In the swamps it was already hard to keep our balance because of the vines under the water we called "wait-a-minute vines." However, each time I was assigned to carry the M60 or the AN/PRC 77, as I would strap them on, Mark would ask me what I was doing. He would give me that look like, "What are you crazy!" He insisted I give him the equipment and he carried it for me. In my eyes he was not just a big guy, he was a man with a giant heart.

I gained ten pounds in winter Ranger School. I think I'm probably the only person in the history of the Rangers to *gain* weight—I had to just to survive. When I look at that coveted ranger tab, I remember that if it were not for my ranger buddies, I would never have graduated. It took selfless teamwork.

━━━━━━━━━━━━━━━

Great organizations have a history of unbroken teamwork and special bonding. Each Labor Day weekend, the 104th WWII veterans, widows of veterans and family members called "pups," gather in a city they select and spend several days sightseeing, reminiscing old war memories and catching up on the latest news. One of the greatest days of my life was the day I was promoted to Brigadier General in a large ballroom with these veterans, whom I have come to love as family.

One of those veterans lived near my home when we lived in Oregon and we had many special times to talk and swap stories. I've noticed that whenever this humble, white-haired man walked into a room, his presence was immediately felt and it was obvious how much he was respected. Art Sorenson was captured by the Germans in World War II and yet somehow managed to escape. While serving in the 104th Division, he received the Purple Heart from a combat wound. So gallant was he as a warrior, that he was awarded the Silver Star and two Bronze Stars.

One of the main reasons Art is alive is because of teamwork. He recalls the time the Third Armor Division needed to advance from the Ramagen Bridge to Nordhausen. They could not advance without infantry support. So Art and his buddies in I, K, and L companies of the 3rd/414th Battalion put as many as ten men on a tank and rode with them forward. Much of their advances were made at nighttime. Whenever they were attacked, the infantry dismounted and counterattacked to prevent the Germans from disabling their tanks with antitank missiles. On Easter day, Art remembers advancing into a valley where they were ambushed and promptly lost six tanks. But again, because the infantry worked with the armor, ultimately, they were able to push the Germans back and win the war. Those tanks helped keep the infantrymen alive and vice versa.

Art and his wife Bette, Mel, Dick and Virginia, Glen and Marilyn, and countless fallen heroes represent a time in our nation where everyone rolled up their sleeves, made tough sacrifices, and by uncommon determination freed the world of two empires bent on conquest. The freedoms we too often take for granted were purchased through teamwork. But it was not easy.

Today we live in a world where freedom is assaulted by those who would inflict their terror at any time and any place. Terrorists would impose their misguided and corrupt ideology on any and all who oppose them. While the face of the enemy constantly changes as well as the techniques utilized to inflict harm, the need for teamwork is just as necessary. Those who are vigilant and who work well together will always have an advantage!

Chapter Three

Character—The Index Finger

Character: Influences the *nature* and *quality* of leadership.

Character is the summative features, qualities, and traits that form one's nature and reputation. Since it only takes one blemish to tarnish our reputation, we can see why character is so important. Character is about our *being*. Character influences the nature and quality of leadership because it builds trust; the essential foundation of a leader's relationship with those led. Character is built around what we value and hold dear. Before he died, Captain Donald Hiebert wrote a statement that reflects a clear understanding of values. Donny was an Air Force Academy graduate who died in a B-52G plane crash while on a training mission April 11, 1983. He wrote:

> I only want to raise a family, serve my fellow man (mostly young people), give credence to the Gospels, strive for holiness, and be a gentle soul. I'd rather teach philosophy than poli-sci, fly a kite than a B-52, lead my family in prayer than men into battle. And yet, this profession means so much to me.[7]

Secretary of Defense Robert Gates and senior Army leaders were concerned that after ten straight years of combat, it was important to clearly define the military profession. Much of a white paper written to stimulate soldier's input about their profession was concerned with ethics and morality. The reason for this is clear. An ever-present concern for the military is to establish and protect trust with the public it is sworn to defend. *Trust is an essential part of character.* In order for leaders to be trusted, they must be people of noble disposition. For this reason, officers and noncommissioned officers are expected to personally embrace and teach their soldiers seven values which establish character worthy of trust: loyalty, duty, respect, selfless service, honor, integrity and personal courage.

West Point once had a mission statement that read: "It is the purpose of the United States Military Academy to provide the nation with leaders of character." In truth, it ought to be the mission of every institution to provide the nation with leaders of character. When a nation loses its moral compass, we can be sure its descent into destruction will be swift. Today we have a deeply divided nation. I believe much of this divide is explained by the deterioration of character.

Character has a social as well as a personal aspect. It has much to do with what we let others know about us. Do we communicate to others openness to ethical concern, a willingness to discuss tough moral issues, an invitation to challenge our actions by our values?[8] Ethical fitness does not exist in a personal vacuum. If a leader purposely surrounds himself with those who are unethical, he will be challenged constantly to preserve his character. A bright coal does not stay hot by sitting next to cold objects; it needs the company of other burning coal. If we persist in joining the wrong company, we may find over time that we lose our heat and, therefore, our reputation.[9]

Ethical fitness benefits mightily in the right organizational culture. Where people band together to do what is right under the approval of an organization, good things are bound to happen. Conversely, if an immoral culture pervades an environment, there will be continuous pull on those of strong character to compromise their convictions.[10]

It is essential that we recognize that character is reflected in our *being*. So much of our culture is caught up in *doing*. Fatigue, stress, and temptation can, and will, wear down self-control. It is not just moral compromise or surrounding ourselves with immoral people that can create fissures in our character. Constant, frenetic activity wears down our will to be morally resolute. Strong character requires ethical fitness. It is rare today to find leaders who emphasize the importance of rest! Yet the reality is that any organization whose leaders do not personally rest or teach their people to find respite and relax will inexorably wear itself out! Psychologists tell us that self-control is an exhaustible resource.[11]

Most of us, until faced with major disease or physical breakdown, tend to be hard on our bodies. Consequently, in our tired state, we may fail to see the effects on our character. It is often when we are forced to slow down that we understand just how much our life and our character matter. My friend and classmate Dan, following a major heart attack, wears a defibrillator in his heart. For Dan rest is not an option, it is lifesaving. When I emailed him and asked how his body was holding up, he responded:

> The body is tired most often. I am taking naps on a regular basis just because there is no gas available. I must believe that God gives me the strength to do those things He would have me do. I will continue to live until He decides that I have had all the breaths that I should have. And then I will behold those things (that One) that would take my breath away.[12]

Who are your friends? What types of people surround you? What's your nature like? Do you hold to high standards or would you rather swim in the pond of decadence? Do you make the time to replenish your energy and renew your convictions? We have to protect our character. As soon as we began to rationalize behavior that is wrong or to compromise on our integrity, we set ourselves up for failure. Without sound character, a leader's vision may never come to fruition and his or her hand is arthritic at best.

I learned about character growing up watching and listening to my father. First he taught my two sisters, brother, and me that there were three things we were not to do or we would immediately incur punishment: Lie, steal, or treat people disrespectfully. Growing up was more than just following rules; it was also learning to be honorable. I remember two occasions in high school where dad, after traveling to Malaysia, shared stories with us in our home in the Philippines. On one occasion he went jogging down a beach in Penang when a woman dressed in red began chasing him. She was not able to catch him but while he ran it was apparent in his mind that what she was after could only get him in trouble. On another trip late at night, he received a call in his hotel room from a man asking if he would like a woman. Alone and in a place where no one would have known, it would have been easy to compromise and do what he knew was wrong. Instead he resisted and kept morally pure.

Early in the 1980's, I had the privilege of serving as the first aide-de-camp to then Brigadier General (BG) Don Parker. BG Parker was like a father to me in many ways as he did not just perform his job as the Assistant Division Commander of Operations, he consistently took the time throughout our days together to share observations and lessons that helped professionally develop me as a lieutenant. I called Lieutenant General (retired) Parker to ask him to share with us his thoughts on character. This is the story he shared:

While serving as the Commandant of the Aviation School at Fort Rucker, Alabama, allegations were raised that two officers in the aviation course cheated. There was enough circumstantial evidence for then Major General (MG) Parker to conduct an Article 32 investigation. The investigation concluded that the two officers had cheated, but there was not enough evidence to convict them in court. So MG Parker decided to interview the two men separately on his own. One of the officers attended his church, and two respected members of the congregation (one was an attorney) asked if they could sit in when he conducted his interview. Convinced that he was innocent, they wanted to serve as character witnesses for the young man. MG Parker agreed to let them join him.

When the first officer reported to him, MG Parker read him his rights then said, "Think long and hard before you answer my questions. Cheating is bad, but it is more forgivable than lying. If you lie to me it means you have a character flaw." The young man answered his questions and denied having cheated. The next officer came in and was similarly questioned. He too denied any wrongdoing. But in the course of giving answers, he presented new information. MG Parker then called back the first officer and, by carefully using the new information, the man questioned broke down and began crying. He confessed to cheating in his aviation course and, in clearing his conscience, shared that he had also broken the Honor Code at West Point and he felt great remorse for his actions. The two men from his church were stunned and walked out of the room with their heads down.

The next officer came in again and when he learned of the other's confession, he too finally admitted to lying and cheating. In lieu of a court martial, MG Parker asked for both of their resignations from the Army. He then took the extra measure of writing both of their parents to explain what he had done and why. One of the mothers was angry with him and wrote him several letters that expressed her displeasure in the actions he took. She shared that children often cheat in school and get away with it. He wrote her back and explained to her that the military is the one profession that is charged with training people to make decisions that often involve sending young men and women into harm's way. He was training officers to lead men in combat and that he had young sons himself. "I take integrity seriously. In combat, the one thing I want to know is that a leader has no price for his honesty or integrity." He often shared with his sons while they were growing up, "When in doubt, always do what is right!"

MG Parker went on to share with her that a leader who lies demonstrates that he has a price for integrity and will lie whenever that price is met. Such a leader cannot be trusted when people's lives are on the line in combat. Conversely, there is great security and confidence in the soldier or employee who can trust his or her leader because that leader's character is sound. As the mother read MG Parker's words, she took them to her pastor and he helped her see the wisdom and truth in what the general shared with her. She made peace with him and wrote that she wished her son had had leaders like him in high school.

My deputy, Gail, lost her husband to a rapid bout of lung cancer. What made the loss particularly grievous was that he was in great physical condition, a retired Air Force fighter pilot who did not smoke and was not overweight. Bill was a man of impeccable integrity. On his desk was the following quote: "You can tell the character of a man by the way he treats those who can do nothing for him or to him."

One day in July in Chesterfield, VA at a local airfield, Gail and Bill had just completed a flying lesson. They were dating at the time and Bill still had four other students that hot afternoon. When he finished giving his last lesson, he came into the pilot lounge to get her. Gail gave him a cold Coke and they sat down to discuss how she did with the new aerobatic maneuvers he taught her. Bill paused for a moment and took a small note pad from his sweaty pocket. He then asked if she had a pen. She did and after giving it to him watched as he opened the sweaty pages of his old note book and began to write. When he was done a few minutes later, he put the note pad back in the front pocket of his shirt.

"Bill, what are you writing in your note pad?" He answered, "Oh, I'm just recording each of the ten-dollar bills I received from the students today. He wrote the date, amount, and name of each student. Since they were dating, he wouldn't let Gail pay him $10. She then asked him why he did this. He replied, "So I can record the exact amount of money I earn from teaching flying on my tax forms." She was so impressed by his sincerity, honesty and character, it brought tears to her eyes. She remembers telling him, "Bill, I am so proud to be with you today." He smiled his usual humble smile and then proceeded to critique her session.

The reason I share this story is that too often we relate character to big issues when in reality it is the little things that can make or break us. If we do what we know in our conscience to be wrong by breaking laws that seem insignificant or stretching the truth with others, then we are headed towards much bigger compromises and ethical breaches. Once our character is cracked, we are far more susceptible to ruin.

───────

Effectual character is persevering. It is not some wind-shifted trait that vanishes and appears based on external circumstances. Anne models this truth. The oldest of ten children, I learned about Anne through her sister Theresa, one of my West Point classmates. Anne was a teacher in Guatemala and after working many years on staff in different schools she decided to start a Christian school. Frustrated in not being able to obtain a facility to use, she converted her own home into a place to teach many underprivileged and needy children. Later in life, she became a teacher in California. Despite poor health due to post polio syndrome, Anne works hard to educate children—and not just in the classroom.

Anne became concerned that the town in which she worked, Santa Ana, did not celebrate the Fourth of July. So she worked hard organizing volunteers so that this omission was corrected. For three straight years, Santa Ana celebrated Independence Day. More importantly, her school children learned about the value of our freedom and our nation's heritage. In 2010, a Hispanic man who did not like the fact that the city was now recognizing and celebrating the 4th of July, opposed Anne's work and, through a dishonest video interview in which he selectively edited content, attempted to make the organizers appear racist. By threatening to mount a protest, this individual successfully intimidated the City Council to postpone awarding a certificate of recognition for Anne's group. Furthermore she was accused of being part of a "hate group."

Rather than back down, Anne personally addressed the City Council and chastised them for not investigating the facts behind the charges of racism. Instead of caving in to the pressure of a man with a misguided agenda who did not represent the views of most citizens, she boldly held to her convictions. Along with her many supporters, she pledged to continue working to ensure the city could celebrate an important holiday. Along the way she modeled for her class the value of holding fast to one's core values.

Chapter Four

Attitude—The Middle Finger

Attitude: Influences the *spirit*, *will*, and *force* of leadership.

"He was my gunny, sir. He was a really good man. He was my hero—not just for the way he died, but for the way he lived."—Lance Corporal Mejia[13]

Attitude is the mental and emotional view and mood applied to people, things, or circumstances. Attitude, as expressed, reveals your hopes, values and beliefs. Attitude is the fuel. It influences the spirit, will, and force of leadership. Without the right attitude, leaders can both fail to inspire others and personally succumb to the challenges life offers. Internally, strong leaders strive to do their best; adaptive to change, resilient to adversity. Externally, strong leaders convey a positive, can-do spirit to encourage and inspire.

Humility is a key virtue when it comes to attitude. Humble leaders breed trust and create a place that is safe for employees to grow and work. Conversely, leaders who always have to be right and who demonstrate an attitude of superiority alienate their employees and create resentment. John Ruskin said, "I believe the first test of a truly great man is in his humility."[14] We learn from many leaders what to do or not to do but we grow the most under humble leaders.

Humor is a wonderful technique for dissolving bad attitudes. Many times an atmosphere permeated by fear, sarcasm, paranoia, anger, critical words or ill will can be reduced enormously by leaders who are able to initiate wit or comedy that breaks the tension. Strong leaders have enough backbone and fiber to know when it is wise to poke fun at themselves in order to raise the spirits of those around them. Similarly they know what persons can be called upon to inject humor when spirits are low.

Often there is humor to be found in many situations. I'll never forget the time my family was out fishing and my dad was using a fly rod. As he was casting the line and whipping it back he accidently embedded the hook in his chin. We were immediately concerned at his predicament. Instead of getting mad or worrying about it, he joked with us and a slightly tense situation turned into a funny incident.

Earlier we noted that rest is an important component to protecting our character. In a similar manner, exercise is vital in helping our state of mind. Physically, we find that the better our bodies are conditioned because of exercise, the stronger and healthier our attitudes are. If we do not get enough sleep or the exercise our bodies need, it is easier to become critical towards people and projects. Keeping our bodies in shape involves eating the right food, resting properly and exercising. Personally, I find that if I work out several times a week and on days when I am not running take my dogs out for a vigorous walk, my blood pressure is normal, I *feel* strong, and I generally have an upbeat, positive attitude. Strong leaders recognize the need to stay in shape and work hard to create good habits that will keep them fit for life!

General George C. Marshall was arguably one of the great leaders in U.S. history. Despite his amazing organizational skills, it was his attitude that helped propel his success. Marshall, writing to a VMI professor in 1920, counseled:

> When conditions are difficult, the command is depressed, and everyone seems critical and pessimistic, you must be especially cheerful and optimistic ... The more alarming and disquieting the reports received or the conditions viewed in battle, the more determined must be your attitude.[15]

Jerry is a remarkable leader who, by his very presence, can brighten the atmosphere of a room. When he laughs his whole body laughs. Yet, I would guess that Jerry is an introvert because most of the time he is quiet and reflective—rather serious in disposition.

Jerry lives in Jos, Nigeria, and one evening while his wife and daughter happened to be in Rwanda, several men pulled up to his home in order to rob it. They probably thought Jerry was away traveling. Nevertheless, when they discovered him in the home they were undeterred from their task, and Jerry nearly died because of their malevolent actions. One would think after a severe beating and theft of everything of value, that the victim might become bitter and fearful. Not Jerry.

Each day this leader goes about helping people improve their lives. He does not let the past affect his future. The presence of evil people does not slow down his drive to serve. His attitude is stellar because he chooses to trust God and to rise above adversity. Jerry surrounds himself with like-hearted leaders dedicated to serving others while maintaining a humble and cheerful spirit. Despite living in a dangerous city, these leaders know how to live life to the fullest.

You can imagine why I look forward to communicating with Jerry and his band of brothers. They excel because they positively live out their faith inspired by the Scripture which says, now the nation of Turkey. "And whatever you do, in word or in deed, do everything in the name of the Lord Jesus, giving thanks to God the Father through Him" (Colossians 3:17).[16]

I asked my West Point classmate and good friend Greg, who is a business coach, if he would share a positive example of the importance of attitude. Greg sent the following story:[17]

On Nov 13, 2010, Marine Lieutenant General (LtGen) John Kelly gave a speech to the Semper Fi Society of St. Louis. This was four days after his son, Lt. Robert Kelly, USMC was killed by an improvised explosive device (IED) while on his third combat tour. LtGen Kelly spoke about the dedication and valor of the young men and women who step forward each and every day to protect us. Not once did the grieving father mention the loss of his own son. He closed his message with the moving account of the last 6 seconds in the lives of two young Marines who died with rifles blazing to protect their brother Marines.

On April 22, 2008, two Marine infantry battalions, 1/9 "The Walking Dead," and 2/8 were switching out in Ramadi with one battalion going stateside while the other was just starting its seven-month combat tour. Representing each battalion, Corporal Jonathan Yale and Lance Corporal Jordan Haerter, 22 and 20 years old respectively, assumed the watch together at the entrance gate of an outpost that contained a makeshift barracks housing 50 Marines. The same ramshackle building was also home to 100 Iraqi police; allies in the fight against the Al Qaeda in a city that once held distinction as the most dangerous metropolis on earth.

Corporal Yale grew up a poor, mixed-race kid from Virginia. Back home he supported a wife, daughter, mother and sister who together lived under one roof. He did this on a yearly salary of less than $23,000. Lance Corporal Haerter, in contrast, was a middle class young man from Long Island. These two soldiers, forged in the same crucible of training, were brothers as close, or closer, than if they were blood brothers.

The mission orders they received from the sergeant squad leader probably went something like: "Okay you two clowns, stand this post and let no un-authorized personnel or vehicles pass. You clear?" In all likelihood, Yale and Haerter rolled their eyes and said in unison something like: "Yes Sergeant," with just enough attitude that made the point without saying the words, "No kidding sweetheart, we know what we're doing." They then relieved two other Marines on watch and took up their post at the entry control point of Joint Security Station Nasser, in the Sophia section of Ramadi, Al Anbar, Iraq.

A few minutes later a large blue truck turned down the alley way, perhaps 60-70 yards in length, and sped its way through the serpentine of concrete jersey walls. The truck stopped just short of where the two were posted and detonated, killing them both instantly. Twenty-four brick masonry houses were damaged or destroyed. A mosque 100 yards away collapsed. The truck's engine came to rest two hundred yards away, knocking most of a house down before it stopped. Explosive experts calculated the blast was made of 2,000 pounds of explosives. Yet, because these two young infantrymen didn't have it in their DNA to run from danger, they saved 150 of their Iraqi and American brothers-in-arms.

There were no American witnesses to the event, just Iraqi police. General Kelly concluded if there was any chance of finding out what actually happened so he could decorate the two Marines and acknowledge their bravery, he would have to investigate and submit a request above his signature. So he traveled to Ramadi and spoke individually to a half-dozen Iraqi police, all of whom told the same story. They said, "We knew immediately what was going on as soon as the two Marines began firing." Some of them also fired, and then they all ran for safety just prior to the explosion. All of them survived. Many were injured, some seriously. One of the Iraqis with tears welling up confided that they fled like any normal men would to save their lives. "What he didn't know until then," he said, "and what he learned that very instant, was that Marines are not normal." Choking past the emotion he said, "Sir, in the name of God no sane man would have stood there and done what they did. No sane man. They saved us all."

What General Kelly didn't know at the time, and only learned a couple of days later after he wrote a summary and submitted both Yale and Haerter for posthumous Navy Crosses, was that one of the security cameras, damaged initially in the blast, recorded some of the suicide attack. It happened exactly as the Iraqis described it. It took exactly six seconds from when the truck entered the alley until it detonated.

Putting himself in their heads, LtGen Kelly supposed it took about a second for the two Marines to separately come to the same conclusion about what was going on once the truck came into their view at the far end of the alley. With no time to talk it over, or call the sergeant to ask what they should do, they could only know their orders to let no unauthorized vehicle through. The two Marines had about five seconds left to live.

It took another two seconds for them to raise their weapons, take aim, and fire. By this time, the truck was halfway through the barriers and gaining speed. Here, the recording showed a number of Iraqi police, some of whom had fired their rifles, now scattering—some running right past the Marines who had three seconds left to live.

For another two seconds, the recording shows the Marines' weapons firing non-stop. The truck's windshield exploded into shards of glass as their rounds took it apart and, as the General recounted, "tore into the body of the SOB who is trying to get past them to kill their brothers, American and Iraqi, bedded down in the barracks totally unaware of the fact that their lives at that moment depended entirely on two Marines standing their ground."

The recording shows the truck careened to a stop immediately in front of the two guards. In all of the instantaneous violence, Yale and Haerter never hesitated. By all reports and by the recording, they never stepped back. They never shifted their weight. With their feet spread shoulder-width apart, they leaned into the danger, firing as fast as they could work their weapons. They had only one second left to live.

The truck exploded and the camera went blank. Six seconds. Not enough time to think about their families, their country, their flag, or about their lives or their deaths, but more than enough time to do their duty into eternity. Two men in six seconds expressed an attitude so powerful that fleeing was not an option. Duty performed with the highest zeal imaginable saved countless lives.

Aunt Tita Lou would have liked Helen Keller. This Filipina woman consistently models a resilient attitude despite the painful trials she experienced. Years ago, just before her daughter delivered what would have been her grandchild, her daughter suffered a heart attack and she, along with her unborn child, perished. Currently another of her daughters is suffering from cancer. In her seventies, Tita runs a guesthouse in Los Banos, Philippines. As if it is not enough to consistently bring people into her home and feed them, she adopted a five-year old girl living on the streets near her home. While she raises this girl and runs the guesthouse, she cares for her brother-in-law suffering from Alzheimer's disease. She doesn't complain or feel sorry for her situation. She generously helps others. Her attitude is an inspiration to all around her.[18]

———————

Earlier, I mentioned my son Bryan's brain tumor. One day I was driving back from the radiation clinic where he was going through his twice-a-day radiation treatments, and I have to admit I was a little discouraged. My vision seemed all but hopeless and the chances of our son Bryan living were bleak. From the back seat where he was sitting, Bryan piped up, "It's okay daddy, God will take care of it!" I got chills as I turned my head to look at him. My son was not yet four years old. How did he do that?

Attitude. Bryan recognized something at the age of three many adults would have completely missed. I needed cheering up. Instead of feeling sorry for himself, he cared about me. Today Bryan is our living miracle. You can read more about his story in *Something to Think About . . . in Reveration,* a 365-day devotional I wrote to encourage people.[19]

When family, friends, or co-workers say, "don't," "can't," or "won't," push ahead if you know in your heart that you are supposed to press on! Quietly with the firmest of resolve move forward despite the obstacles!

Chapter Five

Conduct—The Ring Finger

Conduct: Influences the *behavior* of leadership.

Core values posted on the wall of Veckton-Dickinson and Company—"We treat each other with respect. We do what is right. We always seek to improve. We accept personal responsibility."[20]

Conduct is the manner in which we behave. As such, it influences the behavior of leadership and, in reality, validates its character. While character is about *being*, and attitude is about *motivation*, conduct is about *doing*. Because of this, it requires leaders to be disciplined. Strong leaders understand that the goal of conduct is *respect* and its fruit is loyalty and esteem. Exemplary conduct is all about treating others the way we want to be treated—the Golden Rule.

It would seem that conduct today is devalued with each passing year. As our society shies away from protecting absolutes, behavior veers toward what is immoral and self-centered. Those who dare to criticize what they sincerely believe is wrong are labeled as intolerant and marginalized as fools. Honoring others is seldom taught or emphasized. The application of kindness is meanly buried beneath the ever-growing roar of a petulant, "me-first" society.

Respect starts early when we teach our children to rise when an older person comes into the room, and to listen attentively when others talk. Respect means valuing others. It is the recognition that we can learn and profit from those around us. It is a quality that builds trust and confidence in a team and organization because people sense they are valued.

Respect means thinking before we speak lest our words cause damage. When we are angry or emotionally charged, we can harm the very people we love or value. Conduct involves more than just *what* we communicate, it is *how* we relate and respond to people. For this reason, listening is of paramount importance. Have you ever had a conversation with someone and felt they were not really paying attention to what you were saying? Have you ever been with someone who pretended to be interested in you but really was engaged in another activity or distracted by other thoughts? I'm reminded of this myself when I think of my wife trying to talk to me when the television is on!

My uncle, Ralph Erickson, spent ten years serving as a grief counselor for a funeral home. While he counseled people, his own wife received care in a home for patients with Alzheimer's disease. Ralph shared with me how he learned that the best way to help people grieving was to listen to them versus trying to prescribe solutions. Weekly within the group, people would share their story. Over time he heard the same stories repeated, yet watched as people found resolution for their pain. The storytellers gained credibility and found strength through relating what they experienced. Ralph found this to be a rich time in his life for helping others who were suffering.

Ralph understood the value of listening because he grew up with a dad who did not listen to him and, consequently, never really knew who he was. Later in his life as a chaplain, Ralph often met with dependents of soldiers who were misbehaving as a means to gain attention from dads who basically ignored them. From what he learned, he was able to dispense valuable insight to his own daughter. Diane worked in a hospital ward. In her ward was a very mean woman. All of the nurses avoided this angry patient and Diane was at the end of her wits trying to figure out what to do. When she called Ralph for advice, he said, "Go in and sit down with her for half an hour. Ask her if she is scared and then listen to what she has to say." Diane followed her dad's advice. Later she reported to him that the woman was so impacted by her taking the time to listen to her fears and hear her story that she transformed from the worst patient to the best patient on that floor.

How we treat people is incredibly important. When we allow people to share their stories and we listen to them with respect, we gain their trust and establish authenticity as leaders who care.

When it comes to leadership, talk alone is cheap. It is action that gives words meaning. If we want people to follow our vision, we have to demonstrate that we care about them. When people see that our conduct is worthy of emulating, they will be far more likely to improve their own behavior. Noble conduct in the final analysis is sacrificial. The ne plus ultra for conduct is the willingness to die for those we serve.

"Do unto others . . ."

Conduct is equally about doing what is right and giving our best effort. When we get hired to a new position it is our responsibility to learn all we can about the new job. This enables us to know what is expected of us and where to put forth the most effort.

When I commanded the Delta Company Maddogs one of my first tasks was to ask my young soldiers to teach me how the TOW anti-armor system worked. Tactically I had to learn how to best deploy the systems in the field but I also needed to know how to put together the weapon and fire it. When my soldiers saw that I cared enough to learn and master what they had to do, their confidence in me as a leader grew. They were quite enthusiastic about making sure I was proficient.

Every six months we were required to take an Army Physical Fitness Test (APFT). We had to complete as many correctly executed pushups in two minutes and sit-ups in two minutes to meet the standard, and complete a two-mile run in the allotted amount of time. If any soldier did not score a minimum of 60 points per event he failed. Now, I could have gone out for each test and settled for scoring 180 points. But that's not what strong leaders do. Strong leaders don't strive to meet minimum standards they go all out to meet the maximum standard. In order for me to max the test I had to perform 77 pushups, 82 sit-ups and run the two mile run in less than 13:19 minutes. Scoring 300 points set a great example for my soldiers because they saw I gave all I had. It inspired them to do the same and made it clear that Maddogs did not settle for average or below average results.

We don't want to be leaders who are lazy. We don't want to be leaders who are uncertain about what to do or who lack proficiency. Our conduct should reflect expertise combined with superb effort. "Do your best" is a great adage to remember! It is pretty hard to fault a leader who gives all he can.

My West Point classmate, Bill York, as a young lieutenant, served with an air defense unit in Germany. On one occasion, they were training in the largest maneuver area in Germany called Hohenfels. The ground was muddy and for reasons unexplained to him, they had to extend their time in the field an extra two days. To fill the time, Bill set up armor recognition classes in a tent. Unfortunately, the soldiers kept falling asleep during his class which was quite frustrating! So Bill went out and found a tear gas canister. He came back into the tent and in front of all the students pulled out the safety pin. Then he handed the canister to a soldier in the front row and told him and his two adjacent mates to keep awake. If the soldier let go of the spindle the grenade would release the gas.

As one could imagine, for two whole classes this technique worked quite well. But during the third class the unlucky soldier picked to hold the canister, succumbed to heavy eyelids and dropped the grenade. Immediately the spindle popped free causing a fast expulsion of tear gas into the tent. Every soldier was now awake and with reckless abandon, choking coughs, and flailing arms made their escape. Poor Bill had to find the canister and get it out or it would render their tent useless. Naturally, this meant he got the worst of the tear gas!

Bill's ability to think of creative solutions to ordinary problems suits him well. Today he runs his own business as a headhunter (not a cannibal!). Bill helps those who are looking for jobs find employment. When Daniel, a junior officer, was wounded and paralyzed from the chest down in Iraq, several academy graduates and classmates called on Bill to see if he could help this wounded warrior find work. Bill visited him at the Veteran's Hospital in Houston. He noticed that Daniel's arms were caked with dried blood and asked him what in the world happened. Daniel's wife explained that he had been playing wheel chair basketball. He was so competitive that, despite his condition, he spent hours competing from his wheel chair. Because he had no control of his abdominal muscles, when Daniel tried to shoot the ball he would fall out of the wheel chair thus scraping his arms so badly they bled.

By understanding the temperament and amazing attitude of this young warrior, Bill put his networking skills to work and not only landed a great job for Daniel working as an Oil & Gas Trader, he also managed, through some innovative friends, to score him a Toyota 4Runner specially equipped so Dan could drive it.

Eating dinner with Bill is a great adventure. The man is full of stories and while that may not be so unusual, what comes through loud and clear is his love for people. The fact that Bill is a successful businessman is no surprise. Consider his background. He was recruited to West Point to play football. While at the academy he played four sports. Bill loved competing. To him, the journey was just as fun as the outcome. When he left the Army after five years, he joined a small computer company in Houston at the perfect time and rode with it as it grew astronomically. Later, he joined another small North Carolina bank that soon became the largest bank in the US (Bank of America).

Handsome, popular and cocky, Bill was used to winning and to living life to the fullest. So why didn't he become like so many people I have met through the years who when blessed with success become prideful and disdainful of those around them with lesser skills? I did not ask him this question. What I know is that he lost one of his best friends and a fellow classmate, to a horrible helicopter crash. I know he has seen the effect of pain and misfortune on the lives of those who are friends. I know that he recognized in his own life that he had become spiritually stagnant and was just "going through the motions." Pain and suffering have a way of bringing life into sharper focus.

In the great journey of life, Bill recognized what was most important was not that he could outperform most people, but rather that he could lift up those who were in need. Instead of focusing on his own desires and concerns, he has made it his passion to help others. He genuinely cares for people and, watching him at work in his office, it is obvious that he has a gift for making everyone around him better. In short, Bill is a beloved man because he is a loving man. Excellent conduct left to itself may bring success but excellent conduct with care for others creates a legacy.

While serving as the Commander of the 104th Division, I was blessed to have three outstanding Brigade Commanders. One of them, David Francavilla, is one of the most generous men I have ever met. He possesses an uncanny ability both to give and to bring out the best in those he leads. I believe much of this can be attributed to his behavior. There is a key reason why David builds up all those around him. Fortunately for us, he shared with me his story. Early in his life he learned a powerful lesson about how to treat people. As a senior in high school, David was courted by several well-known universities to play football. Even Notre Dame, the number one rated school in the nation at the time, expressed a strong interest in recruiting him. It felt good to be scouted by schools that wrote letters, called him at home, and treated him and his family to dinners. Soon his chest and head were massively swollen with pride.

A small school with only about 1,000 students called David. The coach wanted to take him to dinner. The college had a good academic reputation but its football team was, at best, average and unknown. David was not interested in playing for them. He remembers telling his dad that his high school team was better than their college team and that his graduating class was larger than their whole school and he was going to let their coach know these things. The arrogant words that flowed from his mouth soured his father's face and filled his eyes with disappointment. David's dad sat him down and they had a powerful conversation about respect, courtesy, and responsibility. He ensured David knew that no one should be less noble, less kind, and less true for having been a fellow traveler in life.

So David met the coach and had a fun evening with a man not all that much older than he was. He almost signed a letter of intent with him that night but ultimately ended up playing for a school closer to home. Later, in college, David found that he was not so special after all; there were a lot of big, strong, and fast guys and it was tough to get playing time.

In David's junior year, a new defensive coordinator arrived at the school. After a hard first day of practice, the team got in a line to shake the new coach's hand. As David approached him, the man greeted him by name with a huge smile on his face. Incredibly, it was the same coach from the small team he initially disdained. Because David did the right thing and treated this man with respect, he now had a coach who in turn valued him and made a difference in his football experience. That lesson marked him. Today, David inspires those around him because he treats each person as important. His soldiers love serving with him and would follow him to any battle zone.

Becky Halstead is a motivational speaker in great demand across the country. Becky wrote a book entitled, *24/7 The First Person You Must Lead Is You*. It is a book that shares her story and offers many lessons on leadership. After reading her book, I realized that in the first edition of this book I failed to give discipline its proper due, yet, it is clearly a key component for every leader. Discipline affects each of the six essential elements we discuss. A visionary has to be disciplined, or he may easily vacillate between great ideas, or fail to hold the course on a preferred direction. To build teamwork requires discipline in setting aside time for relationships and team building. Discipline is essential in refraining from activity, or speech that would impair a leader's character. The same holds true for attitude. Without discipline it is easy to complain, or to give up in the face of adversity. Wisdom grows and is enhanced by the application of discipline. The more a leader tests her mind and pursues learning, the better she will lead. But I believe the *sweet spot* of discipline belongs under the element of conduct. It is in *doing* that we apply discipline. Discipline is an action word! Strong leaders work hard with discipline to master their craft, to achieve excellence, and to treat people as they would want to be treated.

During winter Ranger school, a technique my father taught me came in handy for protecting my feet from frostbite. Dad is a Marine, (you discover in life there's no such thing as "was" a marine), who fought in the Korean War. Dad's technique for avoiding frostbite was to keep a pair of wool socks against his stomach. Whenever his feet were numb or wet with perspiration, he would change into a fresh dry pair. That faithful habit saved his hammer toes from getting nailed by the breath of a merciless cold. Many men wouldn't take the time to carry an extra pair of socks and keep them dry. Their lack of discipline cost them dearly.

The dictionary gives us several definitions of what constitutes discipline. Let's examine some of them.[21]

Definition #1: Training to act in accordance with rules.

Definition #5: Behavior in accord with rules of conduct; behavior and order maintained by training and control.

Strong leaders don't rebel against rules and authority nor are they just blind followers. Good order and behavior come about by protecting both our attitude and our character by living in accordance with established rules. The reason so many leaders succeed is they humbly recognize that rules or laws apply to them regardless of their position. They don't let how much money they make, power they possess, or their popularity with others give them excuse to bend and break rules they strictly enforce for others.

Definition # 2. Activity, exercise, or a regimen that develops or improves a skill; training.

Discipline is fundamental to our survival. If we didn't make the effort to drink, eat, and sleep right, our bodies would shut down. Discipline is vital for growth. Strong leaders understand this. It is the consistent application of discipline that makes one stellar as a leader. K. Anders Ericsson is known as the father of the "10,000 hours."[22] Essentially, Ericsson found that individuals who reached certain mastery in their craft put in astonishing amounts of time to achieve their level of excellence. Doctors studied and practiced thousands of hours to become great surgeons. Basketball players spent hours of time with a basketball to become wizards on the court. Leaders committed to do what it takes to be better practitioners are disciplined.

In the Army, if a soldier fails to pass a physical fitness test, his record is flagged and he is put on remedial training. If he fails again, (unless there is some mitigating reason) he is removed from the military. If he cannot keep in shape he loses his job. The military does this because it is not safe to go into battle with soldiers who are out of shape. If we want our bodies to be healthy we must work out! Consequently, on every military base or fort it is common to see men and women from all ranks and positions faithfully exercising.

When I think of regular activity, I instantly think of my father sitting in a chair at zero dark thirty (typically 5:00 or 5:30 a.m.). He is reading his Bible, drinking coffee, praying, and writing in his journal. This is how he starts each day for the fifty-eight plus years I have known him. That habit significantly speaks to his creative ideas, to his character, to his attitude, to his wisdom, and most certainly to his conduct. Strong leaders do not have to be complicated.

Definition #3: Punishment inflicted by way of correction and training.

When I was about 9 years old I got caught in a lie to my stepmom, who reported it to my dad. He called me into their bedroom and took off his belt and I thought "O no, I'm really in for it" because he had never used a belt to spank me before. But then he took his shirt off and knelt beside the bed, handed me the belt and told me to hit him. He was going to take my punishment for me. Wow—that was the worst punishment of my life because the thought of hitting my dad was terrible. I never forgot that lesson and it changed my behavior to be a truth teller. That was the best correction I could have received.

We need to have people in our lives who will hold us accountable and discipline us so that we do not allow laziness, bad habits, or any immoral, unethical, or illegal behavior—this protects us as leaders.

#4 Definition: The rigor or training effect of experience, adversity, etc.

Strong leaders use experience and hardships to grow and mature. Disciplined leaders thrive while those who are undisciplined wilt and wither beneath the crush of pain and opposition. Discipline rides experience and uses it to advantage. It presses forth victory out of the seeds of defeat, setbacks and grief. Discipline is not afraid of the unknown, change or threats because it has already weathered each of them and grown stronger in the process.

Nelson Mandela is a great example of a disciplined leader who dared to speak out against injustice, suffered for it by spending decades in prison, yet prevailed and is now upheld as an amazing role model.

In the months and years to come we are going to experience adversity in our nation greater than ever before. There is a clear reason for this. As our society increasingly becomes intolerant of those who hold to absolute values it is rewriting what is considered right and wrong. Those who hold true to their convictions will be sorely tested. For example, on many campuses leaders known for their conservative views are banned from speaking. Those who express their convictions, if they are in opposition to popular or legislated sentiment, are in danger of losing their job, getting fined or imprisoned, or, at the least, experiencing public ridicule.

After living in Oregon for twenty-four years, it was quite a change moving to Colorado. When I go out to run there is a drastic difference. Somebody stole the air and gravity seems stronger! In order to acclimate and run further I have to go out and push my body well past its comfort zone. It is harder to run in the mountains, but it makes running at sea level easier.

If we will train for the unexpected and push ourselves out of our comfort zone, we will be able to face turmoil and tragedy. When we are in the thick of conflict discipline enables us to control our temper, to refrain from raising our voices, making threats, or resorting to profanity. Discipline teaches us to think before we speak and to listen before we judge. No matter how dark the storm clouds grow, we have the chance to endure and succeed if we remain disciplined.

As a leader I don't always do the things I should do and I don't always resist the things I shouldn't do. I suspect the same is true for you. The need for discipline should encourage us not to try and get through life on our own. Through discipline we make the time to build friendships and we work to communicate more clearly. We realize we are better when we are part of a team. Just being accountable means that when I am weak I have the help of others who are strong.

Now back to Becky. Becky and I were in the same West Point class, although I did not have occasion to get to know her much as a cadet. She holds the distinction of becoming the first female graduate of West Point to be promoted to brigadier general. BG Halstead distinguished herself as a leader in Iraq and with every unit she led. Anytime I run into a soldier who served with Becky, that person has nothing but the highest of accolades for her as both a leader and as a person. Indeed, the more I interact with her, the more impressed I am with her sincerity, her drive and not surprisingly, her discipline.

So allow me to end this chapter on conduct with you, by sharing some of her poignant observations as an excelling leader:

When I practice discipline in my life, everything else starts to fall into place. I make better choices. I respond more appropriately when I am bombarded by events out of my control. It takes discipline for me to stay healthy, respect and care for others, prioritize my time, preserve my character, and maintain my integrity . . . I also learned a long time ago that part of trusting others was having the discipline to not say everything that crossed my mind . . . Discipline touched every aspect of our lives—physical, mental, spiritual, and emotional . . . Discipline defines your character and determines your destiny.[23]

Chapter Six

Wisdom—The Little Finger

Wisdom: Influences the *efficacy* of leadership.

Wisdom is the lifelong application of knowledge with the ability to do what is proper and right. Wisdom influences the efficacy of leadership. By efficacy we mean both the power to produce a desired effect and to give value. Wisdom enhances each of the other essential elements strong leaders master. Going further, we first recognize that *gaining wisdom will better enable us to personally grow and mature as leaders.*

Spiritual learning is an essential aspect of amassing wisdom. Each year I make it a practice to daily read my Bible. I find that it is amazingly relevant to life. It is provocative. It gives me wisdom, hope, people to emulate, and solutions to all of life's challenges. The Bible is the world's all-time bestseller for a reason. It contains powerful and effectual truths that are transformational. The more I learn about God and people, the more I see my own shortcomings and the need for His help to be a better leader. When I don't spend time digesting Scripture my attitude lags and I am more likely to be irritable towards those I care most about which means my conduct is questionable!

If I had to pick the single most important tool for building strong leaders, I would select spiritual exercise for the purpose of

<u>gaining wisdom</u>. Certainly in my life, nothing else comes close in making so great a contribution. But you will have to decide for yourself what you believe to be most important. The key is, through discipline, to establish a habit or pattern that will enable you to consistently learn and make prudent application with what you have learned.

Intellectually, I have a personal goal to read at least two books every month. My favorite books are those that tell a story or stories. If I'm going to be a better leader, I must broaden my mind! Leaders with a fixed mindset, rely upon talent and what they already know to be successful. This leads to fear of making mistakes and breeds insecurity. We want to be leaders with a growth mindset.[24] This means we are constantly seeking to learn and to improve. What good is a leader who quits learning? I'll tell you that such a person is about as valuable as a winter coat in a Florida heat wave! Conversely, you can put great stock in leaders who are consistently learning.

To further emotional growth, I find it is helpful to participate in a club or a home group that meets to study different topics or to play games. Socializing helps us become more adept at learning how to read and treat people. We experience what it means to share emotional highs and lows. Effective leaders circulate among people. We discover that even those who consider themselves to be introverts and who don't necessarily enjoy mingling with people, still make the time and effort to do so because of the gained rewards.

Physically, if you are able, join a sports club or team. We find out what people are truly like when we see them operate in the thick of competition. I once got in a heated argument on an indoor soccer field with another man named Dan. When he went to his sideline, his teammates told him I was a pastor. While he completely disagreed with my arguments, he instantly liked me. Why? Because in his mind I was authentic and willing to rigorously engage in tough competition. Dan later became my associate pastor and one of my closest friends. We didn't just share over a decade of playing soccer together; we spent a lot of time after games learning more about our opponents, teammates, each other, and life.

Some of the best leaders in the world seem to have a knack for storytelling. Jesus, for example, was famous for speaking in parables. Stories are an excellent source for communicating lessons and for amassing wisdom. I'm fairly confident that when you were a child you loved hearing fables and tales. If you are a parent, you probably have already figured out the best way to teach your children lessons that will help them live wisely is by reading or telling them stories. It is amazing to me the wealth of learning that we can amass just listening to the accounts of those who went before us and those living in our midst. Farsighted leaders use stories as a basis for imparting lessons and for keeping the attention of their audience.

Second, *gaining wisdom helps us better understand, care for, and develop those we serve.* While serving as a lieutenant colonel one of my jobs was deputy in charge of operations. Twenty-seven people worked in the section with me and so I created a form to learn as much as I could about them. I took each person's picture so I could quickly put a name with a face. In the process of interviewing each team member, I met Chris, a mature captain. Chris spoke four languages, was a talented salesman, and displayed all the traits one would expect to see in a superb leader. Chris loved to take on challenges. No matter what job he was assigned he not only excelled, he also had a knack for inspiring everyone around him. He consistently worked at furthering his education. I'm not sure when he ever slept!

By getting to know Chris, I was able to harness his strengths and our organization was rewarded in the process. Many years later, I recommended him to my boss for promotion to a key position. He was hired. Later he would go on to become a senior executive in multiple training divisions, earn his doctorate, and continue to get promoted as a reserve officer. Wisdom is indispensable in helping us know others so that we become better servant-leaders.

Third, *wisdom equips us for solving problems, optimizing resources, and overcoming those challenges that can cripple or undermine organizations.* It gives us the ability to understand and move beyond setbacks, disappointments, adversity and failures. Wisdom does not whisper to us to give up when times are tough. Challenges that are understood should not hamstring us. They should propel us to react with measured resolve. If the size of the problem increases, so should the magnitude of our understanding.

Too often, shortsighted organizations fall into the trap of refusing to allow any type of failure. Yet, when an organization adopts a zero-tolerant attitude towards failure, it in reality creates a risk-averse climate where failure is virtually guaranteed! Companies that constantly seek to "play it safe" are not set up to adapt and thrive in an ever-changing, increasingly complex world.

When I serve as a guide to organizations that come to West Point through the Thayer Leader Development Group (TLDG), one of the topics of discussion at Trophy Point is about Captain Thomas Machin. Thomas was the engineer who designed the great chain from 1776 to 1778. The purpose of that chain was to block British warships from traveling on the Hudson River in the vicinity of West Point, a strategic fort that George Washington was keen on defending. In the spring it was attached to logs and deployed across the river. In the fall, before the river could freeze, it was removed. When the chain was first deployed across the river it failed.

Instead of firing Captain Machin for a deficient product, George Washington and Governor Clinton gave him a second chance. They recognized that the young officer was sharp and had given his best. Thomas did not disappoint them. He improved the design of the chain. He doubled the size of the links from 1.25 to 2.5 inches. He created a clevis to make the chain more manageable by section and, he created a swivel, so that it could survive the strong Hudson current that snapped the first chain.

Chip and Dan Heath noted in their book *Switch*, "The growth mindset, then, is a buffer against defeatism. It reframes failure as a natural part of the change process. And that's critical, because people will persevere only if they perceive falling down as *learning* rather than *failing*."[25] Failure is a natural part of life. We all eventually fail and die. Therefore, to remove people who fail in the course of their work is to deprive an organization of the opportunity to learn from mistakes and improve.

The problem is not really failure. The problem is *repeated* failure. When a person is lazy, stubborn, or apathetic, and repeats a mistake or persists in not meeting the standard, then there is good reason to relieve him. When a person willfully violates law or well-established standards, that is a failure that probably justifies termination.

Third, *wisdom ensures the moral compass remains on "true north."* By knowing and doing what is just and right, strong leaders possess an incalculable worth and protect their organization from moral failure even if progress is jeopardized by the preservation of truth. When we choose to value and protect what is true, we create a safe organization where people and time-established principles are placed above fads, knee-jerk cultural pressures, and the ever-seductive call of money, power, and prestige. Beware of acquiring relevancy at the expense of integrity. It is never worth it.

A college president may believe she made her campus relevant by creating safe spaces where students may openly discuss and disagree on issues. But if those safe spaces mean that the majority of campus is off-limits to controversial topics and, bans those who dare speak their convictions, I would submit that students first amendment rights are corrupted on the altar of protecting peoples' feelings—a most illusory and mind-numbing practice. We don't make stronger leaders by shielding people from controversy. We make stronger leaders by insisting on rigorous debate, expanding our minds and hearts, and developing thicker skins. An effective moral compass by definition must protect absolutes. If it does not, it will spin towards the nearest popular magnet and eventually the most appeased will be the most lost.

Are you a learner? Are you growing in wisdom? *One of the best things we can do for our organization is to grow personally.* If we think about it, there are all kinds of things that have happened in our lives that caused us to learn. The day we stop learning is the day we should stop leading. I hope that day never comes in my life or your life! Great leaders are lifelong learners.

One of my favorite personal stories I like to share with listeners is about an experience I had as a young company commander in the 101st Airborne Division (Air Assault). When I took over Delta Company its nickname was Delta Death. This was in part because it was an anti-armor company in an infantry battalion and Fort Campbell, where we were located, was mostly forested in its training areas and was not a good place to employ our tank-killing missiles. Consequently, Delta was consistently given tasks like cleaning the battalion area, painting, and other demeaning assignments that did nothing to build morale. I agreed to take command of the company if the Battalion Commander, Johnny Gilreath, would stop assigning the company these tasks. To his credit he agreed and kept his word.

My first task was to change the culture of the company from frustration and a defeated attitude to one of excitement and opportunity. So we had a naming contest. The soldiers elected to rename our company the Maddogs. One of the soldiers created a beautiful mural with a fierce-looking dog. Next, I brought in my yellow Labrador retriever, Dusty, to be our company mascot. She was anything but fierce, but the soldiers loved her—especially when she accompanied us on our 25-mile foot marches.

On one occasion on a beautiful sunny day, I was tasked to be an observer of Alpha Company, which was out in the woods conducting training. With Dusty in the back of the jeep eagerly wagging her tail, I drove out to the training area where Alpha was supposed to be. After shutting the jeep's engine off, I got out of the vehicle and climbed a pine tree in order to see where Alpha was located. Sure enough, I spotted them deeper in the woods.

With Dusty right at my side, we quietly walked down a dried creek bed. I pulled out an artillery simulator. This is a white cylinder with a string at the top. When the string is pulled the simulator emits a piercing whistle for several seconds before exploding. I pulled the string and threw the simulator close to where Alpha soldiers were setting up a perimeter. Just as I threw it I had a horrible realization . . .

Dusty, thinking we were playing fetch, took off after the whistling simulator. I was sure I had just killed my dog! Fortunately, I threw the simulator a long way and it landed in a stagnant pond near the soldiers. Dusty did not see where it landed as it spun and whistled in the water and then exploded harmlessly. I'll never forget her looking back at me with an expression of "what was that all about?"

Alpha Company soldiers, startled by the explosion, did the right thing and picked up their M16 rifles and started firing their blanks in my direction. Quickly, before I could get captured, Dusty and I took off running and we jumped in the jeep and took off. Two days later a rumor circulated the battalion that the Maddog Company had a dog trained in explosives. I had a great laugh over that, but more importantly I learned a valuable lesson: Think before you act!

Melissa is a wonderful mom with three very active boys! I've always been impressed with her calmness in dealing with stress or the unexpected surprises that come from parenting. When her twin sons David and Alex were about four years old, they would observe their mom driving from their car seats in the back. Melissa turned into a Type A competitive and intense woman behind a steering wheel. When other drivers would unexpectedly cut her off or drive in a way that impeded her she would call them *idiots* and get flustered.

David and Alex picked up on her habit and soon began to call each other idiots or others that they observed. Realizing that this was not behavior she wanted duplicated she resolved to stop using the term. One day, someone again cut her off. This time, instead of using that forbidden word, she grumbled with more of a grrrrrrrr. One of the boys then asked her, "Mom was that an idiot?!"

Language and how we use it makes for lots of learning opportunities. When we speak unwisely, who knows who may pick up and duplicate what we wish went unsaid. Learning leaders are careful about what they say!

———————————————

Juan is a policeman and once served as my Command Sergeant Major in the 104th Division. On a road trip from Houston to College Station, he wistfully recounted the great road trips his family made across the United States while he was growing up. His father was a self-employed truck driver and, on occasion, would tell the kids to pack up and jump in the back of their camper. He would not tell them their destination and that added to their sense of adventure. From their starting point in Warden, Washington, they drove across country. On one such trip, his dad stopped at a gas station somewhere deep in Texas.

After fueling, he told the kids to jump in the camper and then off they went. Little Juan did not see his mother in the front and she certainly was not with them in the back. So he yelled to his dad who, annoyed at the interruption, asked what he wanted. His dad could not hear through the thick window so Juan did his best mouthing the words, "Where's Mom?" His dad thought he was asking where they were going and since that was always a well-guarded secret, told him to quit bothering him. Figuring his dad must know what he was doing, Juan went back to playing with his siblings in the back.

Fifty miles later, a Texas state trooper pulled them over. Casually he walked up to the cab and asked Juan's dad if he was missing something. When his father gave the officer a puzzled look, the trooper said, "You left your wife at the gas station!" Of course Juan's mom's version was much better. She saw her husband driving off without her and ran down the road chasing the camper and yelling at him to stop! He never saw her. He made the assumption she was in the back with the kids. And from that great adventure, Juan learned a life lesson. Be careful about making assumptions!

Lieutenant General (Ret) Sam Wilson is a profound example of a learning leader. Sam grew up on a 150 acre farm in rural Virginia. His parents were readers, and they fostered in their children a deep love of books. Sam's mother, a former public school teacher, insisted that his older sister and three brothers valued learning. She taught them much about discipline, self-control, and how to think logically. Meanwhile, Sam's father was a prolific storyteller. His imagination and ability to turn everyday events and circumstances into stories taught Sam to be observant and creative. By consistently studying, reading and keeping up with current events, it was amazing what he accomplished.

At the young age of sixteen, Sam joined the Virginia National Guard. His leadership skills were such that he was sent to the Infantry Officer Candidate School (OCS). Sam graduated at the head of his class and, upon promotion to second lieutenant, was selected to teach at the Infantry School. By the age of nineteen he was teaching counter-insurgency. President Roosevelt asked for volunteers for a dangerous mission and Sam was selected. He was one of Merrill's Marauders in WWII serving behind enemy lines in Burma.

In September 1947, Sam entered the Army's Foreign Area Specialist Training Program (FASTP) and was enrolled in graduate school at Columbia University. From there he went on to become virtually fluent in Russian and had a good grasp of many other languages. What makes him special is not just that he personally amassed knowledge, but that he had a knack for making any organization he served better. His innovative insight and pursuit of excellence led to his selection to the Army Infantry Hall of Fame, US Military Intelligence Hall of Fame, Army Ranger Hall of Fame, and the Defense Intelligence Agency US Attaché Hall of Fame. General Wilson was also named Professor Emeritus for the Army John F. Kennedy Special Warfare Center & School and was awarded the State of Virginia Cultural Laureate for Public Service by the Virginia Cultural Laureate Foundation. He was the 1994 winner and first recipient of the General Doolittle Educator of the Year Award for distinguished service to Special Operations Education.[26]

General Wilson, despite never attaining a college degree, became President of Hampden-Sydney College and in 2000 he was named President Emeritus. When I emailed LTG (ret) Jerry Boykin and asked if he had someone he could suggest as an example to us of a leader of wisdom, he quickly suggested Sam Wilson. In describing him he wrote:

> He is a lifelong learner who at 87 years old still teaches and studies myriad subjects. When you sit and talk to him, he is conversant on many subjects and can discuss them in fluent Russian. His continual grasp of current events is impressive and he puts things in the context of history.

Doug was the pastor of a church in Arizona. With his spouse and two sons everything seemed wonderful. But one night his wife did not come home. He went out looking for her and found her with the man who was his key helper in the church. He was devastated and did not know what to do. He lay on the floor of his home for days crying. After his wife left him, his life descended into chaos. For several years, he tried to make things work but to no avail. Finally, he found church homes for all the folks in his congregation and then closed the church and left the ministry with a broken heart. Despite the fact that it was his wife who was unfaithful, *he* felt he had let people down. Frustrated, angry with God, confused and depressed, one day he decided to just walk out into the desert and die.

Without telling his sons Bryan and Matthew, Doug walked far into the Arizona wilderness. After several days, he was overcome by the heat and became so dehydrated he could not even walk. He was ready to die yet rationalized that he was not committing suicide because the elements would overtake him. Doug lay on prominent ground and positioned himself so searchers could easily find his body. He didn't want to be eaten by some varmint. He folded his arms on his chest and closed his eyes. All of sudden he felt something tap him. Repeatedly he was touched and he opened his eyes. All around he saw blue sky yet directly above him was a rain cloud. Heavy drops fell on him which he gulped down and then filled the containers he had with him. He was revived!

Two nights later Doug verbally exploded—calling God every filthy word he could think and hurling accusation upon accusation. For what seemed like hours he ranted, screamed, and cussed at God for all his problems. Then he just stopped. In that moment, he experienced a great release. For the first time in a long time he heard the voice of God speak to him. Ashamed of his words and expecting to be struck by a lightning bolt, instead he heard God say, "This isn't news to Me, you've had this in your heart all along. Now that you've gotten it out I can begin to heal you."

Incredibly, Doug survived for ten months in that desert. Fortunately, he was somewhat of a survivalist with firsthand experience in how to live in a desert environment. Now you might wonder what in the world does this story have to do with wisdom? In a profound sense, when Doug was stripped of everything that mattered and left with lots of time to think, his ability to learn was actually heightened. During this period he established with God a relationship he didn't previously think was possible. Drawing from his memories of the Bible and from uninterrupted time to reflect, Doug began to understand how much God cared for him. In the wilderness he discovered his Father's love.

This broken pastor realized there were so many people like him, who were hurting and needed help—not just someone to say, "I'll pray for you," but to actually care. One night while sitting by a fire, he heard a voice say, "536-9325." Several times that number was repeated. He remembered it was the number of a church he once served.

Doug walked out of the desert to a payphone and called that number. He asked for the pastor and was told he no longer ministered there. Finding out his new number, Doug made a collect call and connected with his former pastor, Raymond. He told him his location and shared he was ready to do whatever God wanted for him next. His relationship had been built on material things, his family, and things that were temporal. Now that his relationship with God was renewed he knew he needed to help hurting people.

In order to start fresh, Doug returned to Lawton, Oklahoma where his parents lived. In their church, the first person he encountered was Bill, a longtime friend, and the state founder and director of Teen Challenge. Bill invited Doug to come and work with him. With a grateful heart he accepted and began a ministry to help teens in pain.

Bryan and Matthew were reunited and reconciled with their father. Not a day passes by without Doug remembering the grace God extended to him. When I spoke with him, he shared how blessed he was to be remarried to Carolyn—a fantastic wife and friend! "Promises have to die before they can be fulfilled."

Wisdom is often born through pain. It is nurtured by suffering and matured through grief. Likewise, amassing wisdom can lead to both vexation and sorrow. The wise King Solomon noted, "For with much wisdom is much sorrow; as knowledge increases, grief increases."[27] Leaders who are able to gain knowledge through adversity bring incalculable worth to their organizations. Life does not always go the way we expect. When we are able to learn from our mistakes, the twists and turns of fate, and the actions of good and bad people, we possess the power to discern and to dispense insight.

Chapter Seven

Putting the Hand to Work

The hand is the artisan of the soul. It is the second member of the human trinity of head and hand and heart. A man has no faculty more human than his hand, none more beautiful nor expressive nor productive.

—Robert Leckie in *Helmet For My Pillow*

Definition of a Strong Leader: A strong leader is someone who faithfully unites heart and mind in honorable, selfless action for the betterment of others so as to effectively accomplish the mission.

Strong leaders are selective and deliberate about what they put their hands to and the manner in which they operate them. They not only effectively utilize the six essential elements, they also understand the appropriate style of leadership to execute within their organization. This is where wisdom and discernment are of particular importance. When this phenomenon occurs, we have a condition that is transformational!

Transformational Leadership = Leadership which effectively combines all six elements (vision, teamwork, character, attitude, conduct and wisdom) **appropriately so as to lead an organization to sustained success.**

While it is important to master the essential six elements to effectively serve people and transform organizations, it is also important to recognize there are certain tools that help us become better leaders. There are two tools that I find to be absolutely indispensable. These are tools that can immediately be applied and which, when used by leaders, create healthy organizations.

The first tool is behavioral reading. Created by Dan Korem and extensively taught in his books *The Art of Profiling* and *Snapshot*, profiling gives a leader the opportunity to read and treat people right the first time. Behavioral profiling is based upon correctly reading a person's actions. It is not about their race or ethnicity.[28] Dan teaches people communication types (nonassertive, assertive, control, express) and performance types (fearful/cautious, confident, conventional, unconventional) to help people make accurate reads. These reads are applicable in the work setting, school, family, etc.[29] By knowing how to read behavior we learn how to treat people correctly the first time.

The second tool I highly recommend is *Strengthsfinder 2.0* with the book *Strengths Based Leadership*. In this book, Gallup revealed the results of a thirty-year research project that galvanized people to discuss strengths. Over 7 million people have taken the assessment that reveals their five strengths.[30]

As a two star division commander, I expected my command teams to complete the Strengthsfinder 2.0 questionnaire. This was accomplished by each person buying the book and utilizing the password provided at the end in order to complete the questionnaire on the internet which, when finished, revealed their five strengths in order of magnitude. There are three reasons why this is key: First, by understanding each leader's five strengths, I was better able to mentor each leader and ensure that their strengths were put to use in the military, while conversely also ensuring I was not expecting them to produce in areas where they were weak. Second, we were able to build strong teams in our organization because, when people were encouraged to work using their strengths, their morale went up, efficiency improved, and teamwork was enhanced. Third, this tool helped me better understand myself, which was invaluable in finding people for the team who were strong in areas where I was particularly weak. Take advantage of profiling and Strengthsfinder 2.0 so as to better understand and thereby serve people!

Strong leaders recognize that different leadership styles are necessary at different times in order to successfully lead a team or organization. In this chapter I will share three different leadership styles. Because leaders and the people they serve go through a maturation process, it is unwise for them to lock in and operate with only one leadership style. Differing conditions will warrant differing approaches. One style does not fit all circumstances or environments. Before determining which style to use, the strong leader is wise to understand the condition of the team or organization he or she is leading. There are three things a leader should evaluate in each team member: proficiency, commitment, and focus.

Directive Style

If a worker's proficiency is low (beginner stage) and the team or organization is fairly immature, the leadership style will generally need to be more directive. Generally the less committed an employee is, the more directive the leader must be. The more immature a person is, usually the more self-focused he or she will be. As people mature, they tend to become more aware of the needs and concerns of their teammates. While a person will always have needs, the individual who serves for the good of the team will in the end be most constructive towards team success and harmony. It stands to reason that in organizations where self-focus is high, a more directive style of leadership is necessary.

Young leaders will not necessarily have the experience and maturity to coach, support or empower followers. For example, a new or inexperienced leader would face ridicule or resentment if he tried to coach an experienced veteran. Early on, the leader provides the directives the organization stipulates and ensures rules and processes are followed. In time, as the leader learns how the organization operates, he should become more participatory. Change is a constant with every organization that experiences employee turnover. A mature organization gaining new employees will require directive leadership combined with supportive or empowering leadership.

Participatory-Coaching Style

If a worker's proficiency is medium (intermediate stage) and the team or organization is fairly mature, the leadership style will generally need to be more participatory. Because there is better buy-in or commitment to the organization, a leader does not need to be as directive, but can serve more as a coach. For senior leaders, it is important to help junior leaders mature beyond a directive style to a participatory style. If they cannot make this jump, there are likely serious control issues (insecurities) that need to be addressed. Leaders who insist on micromanaging when the team is already capable of handling its responsibilities will suffer poor retention and face morale problems.

Supportive-Empowering

If a worker's proficiency is high (advanced stage) and the team or organization is very mature, the leadership style will generally need to be more supportive-empowering. With strong employee commitment to the organization, a leader works to empower the employee to maximize his or her success. For senior leaders, it is important to help mid-level leaders mature beyond a participatory style to a point where they can mentor and be available to support as needed. If they cannot make this jump, they will prevent junior leaders from becoming even stronger and emerging themselves to take on more responsibility. Great leaders discern talent and can spot leaders who have the capacity and commitment to surpass them—this is a good thing!

The Transformational Leadership Model

After studying the model on the next page, I will ask you questions to consider for each style. In essence, my hope is that these questions will stimulate helpful interaction and reflection regarding style implementation! The answers or conclusions you reach will be situation-dependent. This, in turn, calls for wisdom since it would be easy to become prescriptive with solutions to contrasting work and employee challenges—just be careful. Sometimes even methods which seem counterintuitive work simply because the leader's hand was genuinely engaged with all the essential elements at work![31]

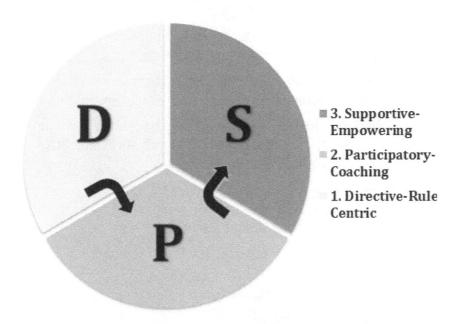

Transformational Leadership Leader Styles

- 3. Supportive-Empowering
- 2. Participatory-Coaching
- 1. Directive-Rule Centric

The Directive-Rule Centric Leader: If a worker's proficiency is low (beginner stage) and the team or organization is fairly immature, the leadership style will generally need to be more directive. The goal with time and training is to decrease the need to micromanage.

The Participatory-Coaching Leader: If a worker's proficiency is medium (intermediate stage) and the team or organization is fairly mature, the leadership style will generally need to be more participatory. Because there is better buy-in or commitment to the organization, a leader does not need to be as directive and can serve more as a coach. With further maturation, the leader moves towards empowering.

The Supportive-Empowering Leader: If a worker's proficiency is high (advanced stage) and the team or organization is very mature, the leadership style will generally need to be more supportive-empowering.

The Directive and Rule-Centric Leader

Key Questions:

1. What are the indicators within an organization that a directive approach is no longer effective?

2. What often happens when a leader remains overly focused on micro-managing or controlling people and systems?

3. High absenteeism and low morale may indicate employee dissatisfaction with the leader or work environment. How might this problem be addressed?

4. How should a leader lead an organization with a mixture of immature, mature, self oriented and team oriented employees that are underachieving?

5. What are effective ways for the leader to test for employee strengths?

6. How does a rule-centric approach actually enhance the leader's ability to lead?

7. How does the leader know when it is safe to become more participatory?

Beware with the directive method of becoming heavy handed, overly controlling, or so dictatorial that followers become intimidated, resentful, or disinclined to work.

The Participatory and Coaching Leader

Key Questions:

1. What are the indicators within an organization that a participatory, coaching approach is no longer effective?

2. What are the dangers of a leader remaining overly focused on working within the team and coaching?

3. What are effective ways for the leader to build employee strengths and mitigate weaknesses?

4. When quality is more important than speed and time is available for the leader to invest in coaching, what tangible benefits ensue?

5. What are potential obstacles that might hinder the leader from investing the time necessary to develop employee strengths?

6. What kind of activities might the coach employ to strengthen teamwork?

The Supportive and Empowering Leader

Key Questions:

1. What are the indicators within an organization that a supportive approach is no longer effective?

2. What may happen if the leader over-delegates tasks and responsibilities?

3. What are effective ways for the leader to reproduce strong leaders?

4. What should the goal be for every strong leader with respect to reproduction?

On three different occasions my job was to start a new church. In each case, I started with small core teams and directive leadership was necessary because everyone who volunteered to join the team needed to know their respective responsibilities and the guidelines that would help us succeed. Because in most cases I was working with experienced adults, it only took about six months to transition to participatory leadership. As a group, we designed and distributed flyers to alert the community to our presence and vision. We brainstormed ideas for serving the people in our neighborhoods. We had lots of fun welcoming and serving new attendees.

After about a year, it was possible for me to focus on my responsibilities in teaching and leading music, while coaching the other leaders. While each church grew and I served with wonderful people, I was never able to move to a supportive or empowering leadership style. The first church ended up merging with another church and I was no longer the senior leader. In the next two churches I passed on my role to bivocational pastors who unfortunately were not able to keep them going.

In a new church, many people come who are needy and require much counseling and support. To prepare for this, it is essential that there is either a large and healthy core group or the ability to bring in strong trainers. The former can usually absorb and naturally help those who are needy, while the latter is able to bring training that brings those in need to a position of health (or referral to another church). Leaders who are strong trainers or builders are excellent at creating structure within an organization that moves people from close direction to the place where they eventually are empowered to become leaders.

Four of my personal strengths fit well in entrepreneurial work—activator, ideation, positivity and strategic.[32] My fifth strength is maximizing, which is somewhat ironic. In essence, I function best when an organization needs to go from good to great. This is probably a strong reason why I thrive within the military. I have always had a group that is trained and merely needs to move to the next level. Unfortunately, with new churches there is often a need to grow from raw to great—a long progression that requires leaders who are methodical builders. I am not an effective trainer/builder. Without a large core group or the necessary trainers and builders, I could not just coach the core team. By default, I also needed to train those who were new and joined our team—something for which I was not well-suited.

Why do I share this? In many ways, the churches I started mirror the challenges business or other nonprofit organizations face. It is important for you to understand your own strengths and limitations so you not only master the six essential elements, but also have a sane appreciation of what styles of leadership best fit your personality and gifting. Don't try to do what you are not best suited for, or you may become frustrated and, in turn, frustrate those around you.

Had I known twenty years ago what I know now, I would have been a much better church planter. I would have looked for builders; people with the ability to take a vision and put a practical plan together to bring that vision to reality. Because I love to create, think strategically, initiate new projects, and encourage others, running my own nonprofit First Cause is rewarding. I am able to maximize our team's work and help other organizations develop their leaders.

The strong leader's hand is most effective when it is used in the proper context with the right styles and perspective. I suspect this will never be easy! I say this because despite decades of leadership experience, I am often reminded of how easy it is to come up short as a leader. While still in high school, my youngest son Stephen and I were engaged in a competitive game of basketball. The score was close when we got into a disagreement over who knocked the ball out of bounds. I insisted he last touched the ball and it should go over to me. Stephen's spirit changed and he quit competing. Eventually, he just walked away and went inside the house. I was frustrated that he quit and so I followed him inside asking him what the matter was. He wouldn't answer me and just continued down the stairs to his room.

Concerned by his demeanor, I followed him and pressed him multiple times for an answer. He looked me in the eye but would not reply. Finally, after assuring him that I truly wanted to know what was in his heart he responded, "Dad, you're always right." And then I understood the problem.

At that critical point I had a significant choice to make. I could say "No, I'm not always right" and, by doing so, validate his observation—because I would be correcting him again. I could argue my case for why I thought my call on the court was correct and in the process further squelch his spirit. Or, I could humble myself and recognize the accuracy of his statement.

I apologized to Stephen for not accepting his version of what happened in the game. I told him I loved him and it was more important to have his respect and for him to know that I listened and valued his opinion than for me to get my way. Had I not learned from my son, I could have ruined my relationship with him. Today, I continue to have a great relationship with all three of my grown children. Each one of them is special and each reminds me that leadership takes work but the benefits are huge!

Strong leaders will fail. They will make mistakes and say or do things that shouldn't be said or done. I know—I've made my share of mistakes and regret things I have done. I hope that you will take what I've learned and improve upon it. Leading is a great privilege. It is an adventure that I hope you will have opportunity to undertake, whether it is in your home, in your community, at work, or at play. Right now, my hand is in the form of a salute—to you! I can't wait to hear your stories! Send them to me at saoleadership@gmail.com.

Six Essential Elements Review with added insights from other leaders:

Vision: Influences the *direction* and *commitment* of leadership.

- ✓ Four important facets related to vision:
    - o *First, it is crucial we craft a vision that is sound and enduring.*

    o   *Second, we have to effectively communicate it.*

    o   *Third, we have to obtain buy-in.*

    o   *Fourth, we must hold it with an open hand.*

Here is what other leaders have said about the union of vision with leadership:

- Rushworth M. Kidder: "Leadership, especially in democratic organizations and nations, is not about tactics, micromanagement, and fine detail. It is about articulating shared values and developing a vision for the future—since that, after all, is how consensus is built and gridlock broken."[33]

- Joel Barker: "Vision without action is merely a dream. Action without vision just passes the time. Vision with action can change the world."[34]

- Warren G. Bennis: "Leadership is the capacity to translate vision into reality."[35]

- George Barna: "A mark of a great leader is the ability not only to capture the vision, but also to articulate it and to cause people to fully embrace it . . . Realize that your vision will reflect your most basic values and beliefs."[36]

Teamwork: Influences the *magnitude* of leadership.

- ✓ First, leaders must lead their team in modeling vulnerability.

- ✓ Second, strong leaders overcome team members' fear of conflict by demonstrating the ability to both allow for disagreement and to teach their subordinates or peers that decision-making is actually improved by inviting dissenting views.

- ✓ Third, strong leaders erase a lack of commitment by team members by holding to goals and established standards.

- ✓ Fourth, strong leaders tackle difficult issues head-on.

- ✓ Fifth, strong leaders "focus on collective outcomes".

    ✓ Sixth, strong leaders work hard at building and sustaining solid relationships.

Read what other strong leaders have to say about teamwork:

- Mike Krzyzewski: "To me, teamwork is the beauty of our sport, where you have five acting as one. You become selfless."[37]

- Vince Lombardi: "Teamwork is what the Green Bay Packers were all about. They didn't do it for individual glory. They did it because they loved one another."[38]

- Michael Jordan: "Talent wins games, but teamwork and intelligence wins championships."

- Bob Taylor: "Building the team is as important as producing the product."

- Mattie Stepanek: "Unity is strength . . . when there is teamwork and collaboration, wonderful things can be achieved."

Character: Influences the *nature* and *quality* of leadership.

    ✓ Trust is an essential part of character.

    ✓ Rest is crucial for maintaining our character.

Read what influential people from the past have written or said about character:

- Aristotle: "Character may almost be called the most effective means of persuasion."[39]

- George Washington: "I hope I shall possess firmness and virtue enough to maintain what I consider the most enviable of all titles: the character of an honest man."[40]

- Abraham Lincoln: "Character is like a tree, and reputation is like a shadow. The shadow is what we think of it. The tree is the real thing."[41]

- Helen Keller: "Character cannot be developed in ease and quiet. Only through experience of trial and suffering can the soul be strengthened, vision cleared, ambition inspired, and success achieved."[42]

- Billy Graham: "When wealth is lost, nothing is lost. When health is lost, something is lost. When character is lost, all is lost."[43]

Attitude: Influences the *spirit, will* and *force* of leadership.

✓ Humility is a key virtue in affecting our attitude.

✓ Humor is a wonderful technique for dissolving bad attitudes.

✓ Physical exercise is crucial in maintaining a healthy attitude.

Chuck Swindoll, a well-revered pastor and author likes to share: "The longer I live, the more convinced I become that life is 10% what happens to us and 90% how we respond to it."[44]

Conduct: Influences the *behavior* of leadership

✓ Remember the *Golden Rule*!

✓ Respect is a key attribute in how we treat people.

o *Listening to people is an important part of respect.*

✓ We always strive to do our best.

✓ Discipline is absolutely essential.

Read what other thoughtful leaders have to say about conduct:

- Benjamin Disraeli: "Circumstances are beyond human control, but our conduct is in our own power."[45]
- Mark Twain: "Laws control the lesser man . . . Right conduct controls the greater one."[46]
- Walter Lippmann: "A man has honor if he holds himself to an ideal of conduct though it is inconvenient, unprofitable, or dangerous to do so."[47]
- Thomas Paine: "'Tis the business of little minds to shrink, but he whose heart is firm, and whose conscience approves his conduct, will pursue his principles unto death."[48]

- Tiberius: "Let them hate me, provided they respect my conduct."[49]

- Alexander the Great: "Remember upon the conduct of each depends the fate of all."[50]

Wisdom: Influences the *efficacy* of leadership.

✓ One of the best things we can do for our organization is to grow personally.

  o *Wisdom better enables leaders to understand, care for, and develop those they serve.*

  o *Wisdom equips leaders for solving problems, optimizing resources, and overcoming those challenges that can cripple or undermine organizations.*

  o *Wisdom ensures the moral compass remains on "true north."*

✓ Spiritual exercise is vital for leaders in wisdom, vision, character, attitude, and conduct development.

✓ Story telling is one of the most effective ways to help people learn!

Here are some poignant thoughts by strong leaders about wisdom:

- Henry and Richard Blackabee: "The best thing leaders can do for their organization is to grow personally."[51]

- W. Bennis and B. Nanus: "Learning is the essential fuel for the leader, the source of continually sparking new understanding, new ideas and new challenges. Very simply, those who do not learn do not long survive as leaders."[52]

- Abraham Lincoln: "I have been driven many times to my knees by the overwhelming conviction that I had nowhere else to go. My own wisdom, and that of all about me, seemed insufficient for the day."[53]

- Thomas a Kempis: "Who is so wise as to have a perfect knowledge of all things? Therefore trust not too much to thine own opinion, but be ready also to hear the opinion of others."[54]

- Friedrich Nietzsche: "The increase in wisdom can be measured precisely by the decrease in bile."[55]

- Piet Hein: "The road to wisdom?—Well, it's plain and simple to express: Err and err and err again but less and less and less."[56]

Wait! We are not finished yet!

As you already know, we can often learn much about leadership by serving or observing weak leaders and, thereby, learning what *not* to do! I encourage you to go to www.firstcause.org/store/productlist. php and order and read next, *The Weak Leader's Fist*.

About the Author

No stranger to leadership, Daniel York directed or led people for the past forty years, to include his current position as the Reserve Advisor to NORAD/NORTHCOM. Growing up in Okinawa, South Korea, Japan, and the Philippines and across the United States, he learned much about leading in different cultures and settings.

Dan graduated from West Point in 1981 and was commissioned a Second Lieutenant in the U.S. Army. He served with the 101st Airborne (Air Assault) Division, and, as an infantry company commander, deployed his unit to the Middle East. In 1986, he joined the Army Reserves where he served as a commander at every level, to include his most recent command, the 76th Operational Response Command. Major General York commanded three divisions—a very unusual accomplishment in the military.

Dan served on staff with The Navigators for ten years during which time he received a Master of Divinity from Bethel Seminary (West) in San Diego, California, before moving with his family in 1991 to Oregon to plant and pastor Horizon Community Church. In 2000, he started First Cause, a nonprofit organization committed to developing leaders (www.firstcause.org). First Cause is active in eight countries.

In 2008 Dan earned a Masters Degree in International Studies. He has written seven books and recorded seven albums of original music. In 2012 he founded VetREST, a nonprofit to help veterans suffering from Post Traumatic Stress (PTS). VetREST is currently forming chapters across the U.S (www.vetrest.org). In 2017 he will launch Strength As One Leadership, LLC a company of senior leaders devoted to providing corporate level and midlevel leadership training (www.strengthasone.co). In addition to this he is a senior advisor for the Thayer Leader Development Group (TLDG) at West Point, NY.

Dan plans on retiring from the military in August of 2017 with 36 years of service. He and his wife Kathleen have three children, three grandchildren and two dogs. The Yorks reside in Colorado.

To Schedule a
STRONG LEADER'S
HAND
Event

Contact us at saoleadership@gmail.com

STRENGTH AS ONE
LEADERSHIP

Source Notes

1. I am indebted to my West Point classmate Brigadier General (ret.) Becky Halstead for this definition modified from her definition of leadership in her book 24/7 The First Person You Must Lead Is You.
2. http://dictionary.reference.com/browse/strong.

Vision
3. http://news.yahoo.com/s/ap/20110406/ap_on_re_as/as_japan_earthquake_warnings_in_stone.
4. Ibid.
5. Terrible Terry Allen, Gerald Astor, (Random House Publishing Group: New York, 2003).

Teamwork
6. http://www.tablegroup.com/books/dysfunctions/the_five_dysfunctions.pdf. The five points come from Patrick Lencioni's book The Five Dysfunctions of a Team. I have preserved the points but amplified upon them with personal thoughts.

Character
7. Contributed by Greg Hiebert, my West Point classmate and brother of Donald Hiebert.
8. How Good People Make Tough Choices, Rushworth M. Kidder, (Harper: New York, 1995), p. 54.
9. Ibid, 54,55.
10. Ibid, 55.
11. Switch, Chip Heath & Dan Heath, (Broadway Books: New York, 2010), p.10.
12. Contributed by Daniel Breckel.

Attitude

13. American Heroes, Oliver L. North and FOX News Channel, (Nashville, TN, 2009), p. 148.
14. http://www.brainyquote.com/quotes/keywords/humility_6.html.
15. http://www.marshallfoundation.org/MarshallonLeadership.htm.
16. Holman Christian Standard Minister's Bible, (Holman Bible Publishers: Tennessee, 2010), p.1590.
17. Contributed by Greg Hiebert.
18. Contributed by Barbara Ennis.
19. To order this book, go to www.firstcause.org/store/productlist.php.

Conduct

20. http://www.bd.com/aboutbd/values/.
21. http://www.dictionary.com/browse/discipline?s=t.
22. The Sports Gene, David Epstein, (Penguin Group: New York, 2013), p.16.
23. 24/7 The First Person You Must Lead is You, Rebecca Halstead, (CreateSpace: South Carolina, 2013), p.74.

Wisdom

24. Mind Set by Carol Dweck is a great book to learn more about this.
25. Switch, p.169.
26. Information taken from two websites: http://en.wikipedia.org/wiki/Samuel_V._Wilson and http://www.stevenpressfield.com/2010/07/general-sam-v-wilson/.
27. Holman Christian Standard Minister's Bible, p. 869.

Putting the Hand to Work

28. Snapshot, Dan Korem , (International Focus Press: Texas, 2015), p.18.
29. I highly recommend buying Dan Korem's book Snapshot to get a basic understanding of profiling. In addition, Dan offers training seminars that can teach people to reach 90% accuracy in profiling.
30. http://strengths.gallup.com/110242/About-Book.aspx.
31. Go to http://www.mindtools.com/pages/article/newLDR_84.htm to discover a great site ondership.
32. These terms are defined in STRENGTHSFINDER 2.O by Tom Rath, (New York, 2007), 41-165.
33. How Good People Make Tough Choices, Rushworth M. Kidder, (Harper: New York, 1995), p. 101.
34. http://www.quoteworld.org/quotes/975.

35. http://quoteworld.org/quotes/1220.
36. The Power of Vision, George Barna, (Regal Books: California, 2003), p. 47.
37. http://www.icelebz.com/quotes/mike_krzyzewski/.
38. http://www.brainyquote.com/quotes/quotes/v/vincelomba151259.html.
39. http://thinkexist.com/quotation/character_may_almost_be_called_the_most_effective/154739.html.
40. http://www.quotedb.com/quotes/1277.
41. http://www.quotationspage.com/quote/29760.html.
42. http://quoteworld.org/quotes/7543.
43. http://www.brainyquote.com/quotes/quotes/b/billygraha161989.html.
44. http://thinkexist.com/quotes/charles_r._swindoll/.
45. http://quotationsbook.com/quote/6800/#axzz1HT9lEwYl.
46. http://thinkexist.com/quotation/laws_control_the_lesser_man-right_conduct/215710.html.
47. http://www.brainyquote.com/quotes/authors/w/walter_lippmann.html.
48. http://www.quotedb.com/quotes/2707.
49. http://www.brainyquote.com/quotes/keywords/conduct_5.html.
50. http://quotationsbook.com/quote/40290/#axzz1HT9lEwYl.
51. Spiritual Leadership, Henry & Richard Blackaby, (Broadman & Holman Publishers: Tennessee, 2001), p.31
52. Leaders: The Strategies for Taking Charge, W. Bennis and B. Nanus, (HarperCollins: New York, 1985).
53. http://www.quotedb.com/quotes/3681.
54. The Imitation of Christ, Thomas a Kempis, tr. by William Benham [1886], at sacred-texts.com.
55. Sämtliche Werke: Kritische Studienausgabe, vol. 2, Friedrich Nietzsche, (Walter de Gruyter; 2nd edition: Berlin, 1999), p.701.
56. http://quotationsbook.com/quote/26722/#axzz1HT9lEwYl.